Setting the Captives Free

Setting the Captives Free

The Bible and Human Trafficking

Marion L. S. Carson

ILLUSTRATIONS BY *Ian Smith*

CASCADE *Books* · Eugene, Oregon

SETTING THE CAPTIVES FREE
The Bible and Human Trafficking

Cascade Books
A Division of Wipf and Stock Publishers
199 W. 8th Ave., Suite 3
Eugene, OR 97401

www.wipfandstock.com

ISBN 13: 978-1-4982-3346-0

Cataloging-in-Publication data:

Carson, Marion L. S.

    Setting the captives free : the Bible and human trafficking / Marion L. S. Carson.

    xvi + 106 p. ; 23 cm. Includes bibliographical references.

    ISBN 13: 978-1-4982-3346-0

1. Slavery in the Bible. 2. Prostitution—Biblical teaching. 3. Human trafficking. 4. Human rights. 5. Slavery. I. Title.

BT708 C188 2015

Manufactured in the U.S.A.

All Scripture quotations are from the New Revised Standard Version, unless otherwise specified.

For the European Baptist Federation Anti-Trafficking Network

So in everything, do to others what you would have them do to you, for this sums up the Law and the Prophets.

—MATTHEW 7:12

Whoever, then, thinks that he understands the Holy Scriptures, or any part of them, but puts such an interpretation upon them as does not tend to build up this twofold love of God and our neighbor, does not yet understand them as he ought.

—AUGUSTINE, *DE DOCTRINA CHRISTIANA* I.35.40

CONTENTS

LIST OF ILLUSTRATIONS

FOREWORD

THE SHOCKING FACTS THAT lie behind this book are that, first, there are more people enslaved in our world today than ever before, and, second, that human trafficking continues to be a blight around the world and particularly in Europe, ruining the lives of vulnerable people, especially girls and young women.

In the ten years of the Anti-Trafficking Project of the European Baptist Federation our member Unions and their churches have made a lot of progress in understanding these issues and, with other partners, taking action on human trafficking in our region. Yet there remains ignorance and prejudice, and in some cases a continued lack of willingness to face up to these evils of our time in the name of the God who created each woman, man, and child in His own image.

Marion Carson is uniquely qualified to address these issues. She is a recognized biblical scholar who has also long been passionately committed to countering the evils of trafficking and slavery in our time. She has been a key member of the EBF Anti-Trafficking Group since its inception, often leading us in profound biblical reflections on different aspects of human trafficking.

Her book does not make comfortable reading. The facts that she puts before us about the extent of slavery and human trafficking speak for themselves. But perhaps even more challenging to us is to take seriously and interpret anew the biblical witness, which has often been seen as, at best, ambivalent on the subject of slavery. By bringing as witnesses the biblical Christians who were at the forefront of the campaign for the abolition of the Slave Trade in the eighteenth and nineteenth centuries, Dr. Carson helps us understand the need for an interpretive "key" to unlock the meaning of the Scriptures, rather than a literal reading on its own—the key here being the over-arching faithful love of God for his creation and humanity, and the redemptive purposes of God as seen in the life, death, and resurrection of Jesus Christ. She also conducts a careful evaluation of the biblical material regarding prostitution, encouraging us to use it to inform our contemporary attitudes as churches.

I warmly commend this book, and its discussion questions at the end of each chapter, to our EBF member Unions and their churches. May it better enable us to be effective in word and action in speaking up for those enslaved and trafficked in our world today, who cannot speak for themselves. In this way may we continue the ministry of Jesus, to "bring release to the captives."

Tony Peck
General Secretary
European Baptist Association
Easter 2015

PREFACE

THIS BOOK IS THE outcome of many years' involvement with groups large and small, formal and informal, who are passionate about ending slavery in all its contemporary forms. It is offered for use in churches, in activist organizations and groups, and by individuals, in the hope that it will stimulate discussion, prayer, and action. I hope that those already involved in this work will find much here to reflect on that will enrich their thinking about what they are already doing. Equally, I hope that that it will encourage many more to become involved in combatting an evil that causes untold suffering throughout the world.

It is not my intention here to describe or prescribe ways in which Christians can become involved. There are plenty of resources available for that, and I have listed some of them towards the end of the book. My purpose is, rather, to introduce readers to what the Bible might have to say about slavery and what is now often referred to as the "sex industry," working on the principle that if we believe that God speaks through the Scriptures, then we must pay attention to what they have to say. But there are pitfalls in such an undertaking. For centuries, Christians believed that slavery was in accordance with God's will, because of what they read in the Bible. History has proved this view to be wrong, but this raises serious questions as to how we read the Bible. Fortunately, ours is not the first generation to face this problem, and we will learn from our predecessors here. As the Abolitionists of the eighteenth and nineteenth centuries knew, if we are to obey God's call to let the oppressed go free, we must learn to discern the voice of love and redemption as we read our Bibles.

The book has been produced specifically for the occasion of the tenth anniversary of the birth of the European Baptist Federation anti-trafficking network in 2015. It has been my privilege to be secretary of this group since its inception, and I have dedicated this book to my Baptist colleagues throughout Europe and beyond who are working against slavery. However, it is not, by any means, intended exclusively for a Baptist readership, and it is my hope and prayer that it will be of use to Christians of all traditions who have a desire to "set the captives free."

Marion L. S. Carson
Glasgow, Scotland
June 2015

ACKNOWLEDGEMENTS

THANKS GO FIRST OF all to the members of the EBF Anti-Trafficking Network whose dedication to combating slavery of all kinds has inspired me to write. At various meetings over the years they have listened patiently as I have developed my ideas on the subject of the Bible and human trafficking, and I am thankful for their encouragement to write them down. It has been my pleasure and privilege to work with Ian Smith, whose delightful illustrations bring the text to life. Dr Julie Green read the entire script and provided valuable insights. She also, along with John Wallace and my husband, Douglas, helped in the preparation of the final manuscript. Finally, I am grateful to Robin Parry, my editor at Cascade Books, for his support of the project.

1

INTRODUCTION

The Bible and Slavery—What's the Problem?

ACCORDING TO INTERNATIONAL LAW, slavery is illegal. Nevertheless, throughout the world today, millions of men, women, and children are sold as slaves to work as domestic servants, in factories, in the construction industry, and in prostitution. The perpetrators of these terrible crimes make huge profits, and the suffering they cause is immense. Victims are tortured and raped, families are split up, and children denied education. How should Christians respond to this? The answer seems obvious. Christians of all traditions are agreed that slavery is unacceptable, and we would be quick to condemn any leader or preacher who ventured to say otherwise. We uphold the United Nations' Declaration that freedom is a human right: no one should be able to view another as his or her property. We believe that no one should be able to force another person to work without pay or by means of coercion and deceit. If we are asked for a theological reason for our reaction to slavery, we say that it goes against everything we understand about our loving God who demands justice in his world. Since redemption is at the very heart of our faith, it follows that slavery is incompatible with all that Christianity stands for. And if we are asked how we know this, we would say that we read it in the Bible.

All this, of course, is true. But unfortunately, the Christian church has not always been quite so certain that slavery is wrong. Throughout much of its history, Christians actively supported and participated in the slave trade, and thought nothing of owning slaves themselves. Not only that, they would probably have said that owning slaves was consistent with biblical teaching. Astonishing as it may seem to us today, it is only just over two hundred years since Christians changed their minds about slavery, and their understanding of what the Bible had to say about it.

The truth of the matter is that both views are to be found in our Scriptures. The Bible does, of course, teach that Christ is the redeemer and that freedom is central to our faith as Christians. The Bible does speak of God's great love for his people, and it does teach us that injustice is unacceptable to Him. But it also contains passages in which slavery seems not only to be condoned, but even to be commanded. Leviticus 25:44–46 contains direct instruction that slaves may be taken, not from amongst the Israelites themselves, but from neighboring countries.

> As for the male and female slaves whom you may have, it is from the nations around you that you may acquire male and female slaves. You may also acquire them from among the aliens residing with you, and from their families that are with you, who have been born in your land; and they may be your property. You may keep them as a possession for your children after you, for them to inherit as property. These you may treat as slaves, but as for your fellow Israelites, no one shall rule over the other with harshness.

In Numbers 31, the Israelites attack the Midianites, and are told by Moses that they should kill all the men and women that they capture, except for the virgins, whom they can keep for themselves (Num 31:18). In the New Testament slavery also seems to be condoned, and even encouraged. For example, in a series of instructions aimed at maintaining good order in Christian households, Colossians 3:22–24 says this:

> Slaves obey your earthly masters in everything, not only while being watched and in order to please them, but wholeheartedly, fearing the Lord. Whatever your task, put yourselves into it, as done for the Lord and not your masters, since you know that from the Lord you will receive the inheritance as your reward; you serve the Lord Christ.

In its exhortation to slaves to obey their masters "wholeheartedly, fearing the Lord," this passage seems to discourage any idea that slavery might not be according to God's will. Furthermore, neither Jesus nor Paul ever says that slavery is morally wrong, let alone suggests that it should be abolished.

If we are honest, then, we have to admit that we have something of a dilemma. How can we believe that God speaks to us through the Bible while at the same time believing slavery to be morally wrong? How can we say that this book, which reflects beliefs that are quite contrary to those we believe acceptable today, has authority in our lives? We could, of course, decide to ignore the passages in which slavery is upheld, concentrating only on verses such as Galatians 3:28 in which it is said that

> There is no longer Jew nor Greek, there is no longer slave nor free, there is no longer male and female; for all of you are one in Christ Jesus.

But this seems to be a rather selective, if not dishonest way to read the Bible. We could, as some do, declare that the Bible is completely irrelevant in the twenty-first century, and throw it out altogether. But this would be to go against centuries of Christian tradition, and indeed, the experience of millions of readers of Scripture throughout the world. The church has always held that the Bible provides us with a faithful witness to Christ, the foundation of our faith, and that God speaks to us through it. Clearly, we have to think things through a bit further, and it is my hope that this book will help Christians do exactly that. Specifically, I want to consider this question: what, if anything, can the Bible possibly have to say to us about contemporary human trafficking? I do this in the conviction that there is an urgent need for Christians to respond to and become involved in tackling modern-day slavery. Just as the abolitionists responded to the great injustice of the slave trade in the eighteenth and nineteenth centuries, so must we respond to the global crime which is human trafficking. But I also do this in the belief that God continues to speak to us through the Bible, and that it therefore must have an important part to play in our thinking about trafficking. If we believe that it is God-inspired Scripture, then we must listen to what it says.

With all this in mind I propose to look at important passages in both the Old Testament and the New Testament to see what they might have to say to us about slavery today. In doing so I hope to show that there is a great deal that can be learned from the Bible about how Christians should respond to human trafficking, and indeed, that we should be doing much, much more to combat it.

Bridging the Gap

Before we do this however, it is important to do some groundwork. The problem I have been outlining—that the Bible seems to accept slavery while most people today think it morally unacceptable—points to the fact that the Bible itself comes from an entirely different age to our own. The life experiences and worldviews of its writers are quite different from ours, and this raises a crucial question. How are we to bridge the gap between the biblical world and the twenty-first century? For most Western Christians, for whom slavery is a thing of the past, it is clearly not appropriate to lift statements like "slaves obey your masters" and apply them directly to our situation today. We obviously cannot condone the idea that we should kidnap people from neighboring countries and make them our slaves, as it says in Leviticus 25, or carry out the command in Numbers 31 that armies in wartime should steal girls to use them as sex slaves. So what should we do with texts like these?

Fortunately, we can look to history to help us in our difficulties. In the nineteenth century, the Transatlantic slave trade was abolished, and Christians played a crucial role in achieving this goal. They believed that buying and selling people to live and work as slaves in Caribbean and American plantations was morally unacceptable, and they campaigned tirelessly to ensure that the practice was stopped. At the same time, however, these Christians also believed that God reveals his will to his people through the Scriptures. How did they reconcile the two views? And how did it come about that Christians changed their minds about slavery? In chapter 2, I will tell the story of how this was achieved. I will give a brief outline of the history of abolitionism and consider what role the Bible played in it. What lessons can we learn for today's fight against slavery? As we shall see, it took a long time, and even a civil war, before people began to change their thinking and believe that slavery should be outlawed. Slowly and painfully, Christians began to see that while the Bible could be used to condone and support slavery, the injustice of it, and the suffering it caused those who were its victims, could not be reconciled with the central truth of God's love for his people and the fact that Jesus' offer of salvation was made to all men and women, regardless of race.

Christians and Slavery Today

Not only do we need help with our understanding of Scripture with regard
to slavery, we also need to have some
knowledge of the current situation.
The achievement of the anti-slavery
movement was immense, but while
laws were changed internationally,
the truth is that there are now more
slaves in the world than ever
before. Certainly, slavery has
always been a global problem,
and we are today much more
aware of its scale than ever
could have been the case in
the eighteenth century. However, contemporary slavery is a far more com-
plex problem than it was for the abolitionists in Europe and the United
States. First, while slavery may be illegal in international law, not all countries are as compliant with that law as they might be. Some governments
turn a blind eye to slavery, and corrupt officials benefit from its profits.
Second, when the transatlantic slave trade could be abolished by means of
law, today the slave trade is a highly sophisticated clandestine enterprise,
and much more difficult to tackle. Traffickers use the internet and social
media to communicate and recruit their victims. They often work hand in
glove with corrupt governments and businesses. It is also a highly dangerous world to try to face, for the gangs that operate in it will go to any lengths
to protect their highly lucrative business. All this shows that it will take far
more than merely changing the law to get rid of today's slave trade. These
problems require concerted and cooperative political initiatives. Of course,
Christians are engaged in these discussions at all levels, and it is essential
that, in addition to their professional expertise, they have a good understanding of why they are doing this work—in other words, that they have
a good grasp of the theology underlying their efforts. Part of the reason
for writing this book is to address this need. I hope to show not only that
a study of the Bible can provide spiritual food for those involved in anti-
slavery work, but also that it has much to say that can inform their efforts
at all levels.

There is, however, a third element in modern-day slavery that makes it quite different from anything the abolitionists had to face. A very large number of women and children are trafficked into prostitution. Their traffickers force them to work in private apartments, bars, clubs, and massage parlors, or on the streets. Of course, this is nothing new, for slavery and prostitution have always been part of the same world. Slaveholders have always felt they have a right to do whatever they want with their slaves' bodies. However, the sheer numbers involved in this trade today make it into something that is a distinctive aspect of human trafficking, not least because of the profits to be made from the prostituting of children. The question is, how should this be tackled?

It might seem that the straightforward answer to this would be that we should abolish prostitution. We might not be able to do much about prostitution in private apartments, but surely if the brothels, sex clubs, and massage parlors, not to mention street prostitution, were declared illegal, and made the target of police activity, then this would go a long way to reducing human trafficking? In other words, if we abolish the sex industry, a large sector of the human trafficking business would be drastically diminished. However, again, the situation is rather more complex than this.

First, not all are agreed that the sex industry is a bad thing, and in fact there is considerable debate about the issue amongst academics, activists, and policy makers. Some think that to make the sex industry entirely illegal would simply result in more illicit, dangerous prostitution, into which many more people will be trafficked. Others think that prostitution should be legalized. The argument here is that if prostitution was to be considered a job like any other, with taxation and good healthcare for prostitutes, then profits would be reduced, and trafficking with them. How should Christians contribute to this discussion? It is a very important question for the reduction of human trafficking. Should prostitution always be declared a sin, and even if the answer is yes, should it be illegal? Might legalizing it reduce suffering?

There is a second factor. While most of us in the West might think that prostitution is wrong, for people in other countries it may be the only way the poorest people can live. In some Asian countries, for example, families find that they have to sell their daughters into prostitution, and for many women this may be the only way they and their families can survive. Are we to take this away from them? Moreover, in some countries a visit to a brothel is acceptable entertainment for businessmen and their guests. In other words, it is part of corporate entertainment. What are we to say about such cultural differences? What all this boils down to is the fact that while the world today is agreed that slavery is wrong, it is not at all agreed that prostitution and the sex industry, which has such a large part to play in contemporary human trafficking, are wrong. It is important, therefore, for Christians to think through these issues in an informed manner.

But there is another issue. Often, Christians have preconceived ideas about prostitution, ideas that can prevent them from becoming involved in anti-trafficking work. While there are many Christian communities and churches that are willing to engage with the problem, many more are too frightened or apathetic to think about it because of its associations with sin and shame. In my experience, some churches simply do not want to talk about it at all, considering it too distasteful a topic to discuss. The problem is, of course, that as soon as sex is introduced to the discussion, all sorts of prejudices and embarrassments come to the surface, and these can hamper reasoned discussion of the topic. This attitude can not only result in ignorance and lack of interest, but in actual cruelty towards those who have been caught up in this type of modern-day slavery. In some cultures, for example in Eastern Europe, it is not unknown for churches to reject women who have been trafficked into the sex trade on the grounds that they have brought dishonor into their community.

Of course, throughout Christian history there have been many who have been rightly very distressed by the particular suffering endured by women and children in prostitution, and have believed it their calling to do something about it. The problem here has been, however, that throughout its history, the church itself has tended to view women in prostitution as shameful, in need of being reformed and punished. Even today, there are many ministers and clergy who take the view that all those caught up in prostitution need to repent, and leave their lives of sin. As we shall see, this is a blinkered view that tends to disregard the reasons for prostitution and the experience of those caught up in it. On the other hand, there are those who feel that prostitutes are "special cases" in God's sight. For example, more than one minister has expressed the view to me that prostitutes are "especially beloved by God." This kind of reaction, although often grounded in compassionate concern, is often instinctive and uninformed, unconsciously influenced by centuries of tradition and cultural attitudes, rather than by anything the Bible might have to say.

In view of this, it is important that Christians be clear in their thinking with regard to prostitution in order to be able to contribute to any discussion on contemporary sex trafficking. How much of our thinking is an uninformed reaction to a difficult and seldom discussed topic? What does the Bible say on the matter? How far can the Bible help us formulate a Christian response to sex trafficking today? The second part of the book will set out to try to help us to find a biblically informed response to the problem of the sex industry and its relationship to human trafficking as a whole.

Outline of the Book

I have been suggesting that there are two problems with regard to the discussion of the Bible and human trafficking. The first is that there is a gap between the worldview of the Bible and that of Christians today with regard to human trafficking. The second is that there is a great deal of confusion and poor thinking on the part of many Christians with regard to the prostitution that is such a large component of contemporary human trafficking. In this book I would like to tackle both issues, and to clear the way for churches to become involved in combatting human trafficking in all its forms.

In order to tackle the first problem, I will first tell the story of the place of the Bible in the abolitionist debate. What can it teach us with regard to anti-slavery work? How did the abolitionists bridge the gap between the Bible and their own situation? We will see that they have valuable lessons to teach us about how we read the Bible. Then, using what we have learned, we will look at the biblical texts themselves. Chapters 4 and 5 will be concerned with what the Bible has to say about slavery in general, and chapters 6 and 7 will be concerned with biblical views on prostitution. In each case, we will conduct a survey of important passages that deal with our topics. However, in each case, we will also pay particular attention to the kind of literature we are reading. For the Bible is made up, not only of many different books by different authors at different times, but also various types of writing, for example, prophecy, law, narrative, poetry, and letters. It will be very important for us to bear this in mind as we try to understand the nature of the biblical texts and what they have to say to us today.

My aim is to encourage Christians to be actively involved in combatting human trafficking throughout the world, and to enable them to have a deeper understanding of why and how they might do this. With this in mind, I have provided study questions at the end of each chapter in the hope that they will help Christians, both as individuals and in groups, to think more deeply about why and how they should respond to the calamity that is slavery. These questions are intended to be used selectively. If you are meeting in a group, you may find it worthwhile to choose only two or three questions to be discussed at any one session. The same applies to the discussion points that are given in the conclusion. At the end of the book, I have given a list of further reading and online resources with a view to enabling readers to explore the subject further.

Before we start our study of the biblical material, however, it is important that we know something of the nature of contemporary human trafficking. So, in the first chapter, I will give an account of the various types of slavery that are to be found in the world today. As we shall see, the problem is a global one that causes incalculable suffering to the most vulnerable people.

2

HUMAN TRAFFICKING TODAY

No one shall be held in slavery or servitude; slavery and the slave trade shall be prohibited in all their forms.

—ARTICLE 4 UNITED NATIONS' UNIVERSAL
DECLARATION OF HUMAN RIGHTS

Human Trafficking: What Is It?

IN HER AUTOBIOGRAPHY, MENDE Nazer tells of her experience of being taken, as a young girl, from her Sudanese village by Arab raiders, and sold as a domestic servant to a family in Khartoum. She had to work seven days a week, without pay. She was made to eat the family's leftover food and to sleep in an unheated outhouse. She was harshly punished for the small-est mistake, and abused both physically and mentally. She was deprived of her personal belongings, and was not allowed to continue her education. Mende was robbed of her childhood, and had the will to care for herself, including her will to escape, beaten out of her. Her owners never addressed her by her name; instead they called her "yebid," which is Arabic for "slave." They considered her to be a non-person, no better than a domesticated animal.

Mende Nazer's story points to the fact that slavery is alive and well, even though it has been declared illegal in international law. However, for many, if not most of us in the West, human trafficking is foreign to our experience. It is something that happens in countries and cultures far removed from our own. We seldom think about it. Occasionally, we will hear news reports of rescued victims, or trafficking organizations being broken up by the police. We may sometimes watch documentaries, read stories like Mende Nazer's, or see films such as *The Whistleblower*, which remind us of the reality of human trafficking in the world today. We are shocked for a while, but then we get on with our lives. Since we believe that we are unlikely ever to be affected by it personally, human trafficking is simply not an urgent concern for us.

In Eastern Europe, Asia, South America, and Africa, however, things are different. There, human trafficking is an everyday reality and risk, and millions of lives are affected by it. It takes many forms. Mende Nazer was sold into domestic slavery, and narrowly managed to escape being sexually exploited, but many others are raped by their owners. Many women and girls are trafficked into the sex industry, and made to work as prostitutes in brothels, bars, nightclubs, and private apartments. Young men find themselves working in factories, mines, or the construction industry for long hours, for little or no pay and without holidays, threatened with violence, and unable to leave. Families find that they have to consent to become slaves of factory or mine owners simply in order to survive. Children are kidnapped in order to be trained up as soldiers, or are forced to beg on the streets. In all these cases, someone is ready and willing to think of other people only as objects, and through deceit or coercion, to sell them on to others to be used as unpaid (or nearly unpaid) labor.

The fact that slavery is not so evident in the more prosperous Western countries does not mean, however, that it does not exist there—it simply means that it is more hidden. In receiving countries (in other words, the countries into which men, women, and children are trafficked) such as the United States, the United Kingdom, Scandinavia, Italy, and Germany, victims live and work away from the public eye, and most people are unaware of their existence. But slaves are to be found in restaurants, laundries, hotels, and factories. They may appear to be ordinary workers, but in fact they are receiving little or no money for their labor, and they, or their families, are threatened with violence if they try to escape. Other rich countries, such as the Arab states, are also receiving countries for people from Indonesia,

Malaysia, and the Philippines who come to work in domestic service, factories, and the construction industry. In the sending countries, criminal gangs are constantly on the lookout for vulnerable desperate people to become commodities. Their victims are made to work in intolerable conditions, unable to escape, and often in fear of their lives or those of their families.

Types of Slavery

According to the United Nations' definition, human trafficking is

> the recruitment, transportation, transfer, harboring or receipt of persons, by means of the threat or use of force or other forms of coercion, of abduction, of fraud, of deception, of the abuse of power or of a position of vulnerability or of the giving or receiving of payments or benefits to achieve the consent of a person having control over another person, for the purpose of exploitation.[1]

Traffickers, in other words, enslave and exploit others whom they consider goods to be used, bought, and sold. They are prepared to use any means to make money, and exercise power over the weak and vulnerable in order to make profits for themselves. They will kidnap, cheat, or deceive in order to obtain their "goods," and use violence or coercion to keep them under control. When the slave is no longer useful to them, he or she will be discarded.

Modern day slavery is generally divided into four categories—chattel slavery, bonded labor, forced labor, and sex slavery. The traditional form of slavery, in which an individual is sold to an owner to become a member of the household, is known as *chattel slavery*. This is the kind of slavery that provided workers for the cotton plantations of the American Southern states or the sugar plantations in the Caribbean until the nineteenth century. Mende Nazer's story shows that that it still exists. However, it is the least common type of slavery in the world today. Nevertheless, experiences like hers are widespread in African and Arabic countries, especially in times of civil war and unrest. Villages are attacked, and children kidnapped and taken to be sold to private owners as their slaves. In effect, the slaves are looked on in the same way as farm animals or equipment—they are there

---

1. United Nations Protocol to Prevent, Suppress and Punish Trafficking in Persons, especially women and children, supplementing the United Nations Convention against Transnational Organized Crime 2000.

to make life easier for their owners, to save them money, and to be used in whichever way their owners think fit. Chattel slaves are most often used in domestic service, although they are also to be found in agriculture, for example, herding animals.

Much more common is **bonded labor**, which is also known as debt bondage. Loans, with interest, are offered to impoverished families who are told that their labor will be considered as repayment. However, in reality, the work they do is never enough to repay the debt. The "lender" is in control of the amount to be paid back, and adds arbitrary amounts of interest. Families have to work long hours, seven days a week. Paid next to nothing, they have no way of knowing when the debt will be paid off, and can remain trapped in this situation for generations. Although the original debt may have been quite small, if a member of the family becomes ill and needs medical attention, or if there are funeral costs to be paid, the debt will be renewed and increased. This means that the amount owed can swell to unmanageable proportions. Bonded labor is especially prevalent in India, Pakistan, and South America. Victims are found in domestic work, mines, agriculture, and brick-making. They are often kept under armed guard, and beaten if they try to escape. Although bonded labor is illegal in most countries, the perpetrators are seldom caught and punished.

In **forced labor**, through trickery (perhaps having been promised a good job) or kidnap, people can find themselves compelled to work long hours in harsh conditions, paid next to no money, and under constant threat if they try to escape. Migrant workers, who have to look for employment in foreign countries because they cannot find work in their own, are particularly at risk from criminal organizations. In some cases, for example in Brazil and Malaysia, hopeful prospective employees sign contracts, thinking they are going to legitimate jobs, only to find that they are being used as unpaid labor in, for example, charcoal-producing camps, mines, or sugar plantations. Forced labor is also known to take place in factories, fishing boats, or restaurants. Employers remove personal documents such as passports, allow workers very little time off, and confine them to their living and working quarters. Frequently, people in this situation are subjected to emotional, physical, and even sexual abuse. They have no pension or health insurance, and they often live and work in dangerous and unsanitary conditions. Their safety at work is hardly a consideration for their "employers," for they are considered highly expendable—there will always be someone else in dire poverty who is looking for work to survive.

In *sex slavery,* women and children (and some men) are enslaved for the purposes of sexual exploitation. For some, this is a result of being taken in by advertisements on the Web for brides for Western men. Thinking that they are going to be married to a rich man who will care for them, they soon discover that they are enslaved. Others are sold into the sex trade and are forced to work as prostitutes. Some are kidnapped, while others are sold by impoverished rural families to work in city brothels. In Thailand, for example, young girls from the north are sold by their families to agents who, in turn, sell them on to brothel owners in the cities. Often the girls go willingly at first, viewing this is as an opportunity to support their families. In countries where there is civil unrest or war, women and children are often especially vulnerable to being trafficked into the sex trade or to being kept as sex slaves for soldiers. In Europe, many girls from Eastern Europe find themselves in a form of debt bondage to criminal gangs. Thinking that they are going to legitimate employment in other countries, they find instead that they are working in prostitution, and forced to give the money earned to their pimps.

In addition to these four major categories, there are other practices that are considered to be like slavery. A widespread but less well-known practice is to kidnap people and remove internal organs, such as their kidneys, to sell for transplant purposes. Child labor is often cited as a separate category. Children are trafficked into forced labor in all the areas we have already mentioned: domestic service, factories and mines, and the sex industry. In Uganda, Burma, and the Sudan, for example, children are taken from their families and trained to be soldiers. They are threatened with torture if they try to escape, and taught to use weapons. The mortality rate is high and the psychological damage done to the children inestimable. In the Philippines, children as young as five work on farms and plantations, and in factories and bakeries. In Haiti, children are often given away by their impoverished families to work as domestic helps in return for their bed and board. Known as *restavecs* (or "stay withs") they often live in harsh conditions and do not go to school. Throughout South-East Asia there is a huge market in young girls to work in the sex industry. Children aged nine to sixteen are trafficked to Japan, Korea, South Africa, Asia, and the Middle East to work as prostitutes. Customers consider virgins to be especially desirable—the younger the child, the higher the price.

Trafficking must be distinguished from "smuggling." Trafficking involves deceit, whereas smuggling means the movement of people with their consent and knowledge of the risk involved with the intention of avoiding immigration authorities. In smuggling, individuals pay others to enable them to cross borders into other countries. Most are looking for work and believe that their only chance is to leave their home countries, without a passport or work permit. Some of these people may well eventually find themselves in situations of slavery, but they do not start out as such, for they have willingly paid (often large sums of money) for the journey. However, if the person involved is a child, the distinction between smuggling and trafficking is dissolved in the eyes of the law. Any child (that is to say, someone who is under the age of eighteen) who pays someone else to convey them into another country will be considered to be the victim of trafficking— whether the child has been coerced into doing so or not.

Human trafficking not only feeds on the suffering of those who are poor, and the corruption of people in power, it is also closely related to other kinds of criminality. Traffickers need forged documents and money in order to enable people to travel illegally. They use legitimate businesses, such as restaurants and clubs, for money laundering purposes, and to hide the fact that the "employees" are actually slaves. They confiscate people's legal identity papers in order to prevent them from escaping. They kidnap their victims and terrorize them by threatening to harm their families if they try to escape. Rape and violence are commonly used to subdue women and girls who are to be used as prostitutes.

Who Is at Risk?

Human trafficking would not thrive if there were not large amounts of money to be made. In effect, slavery affords free labor to those who run illegal businesses. Little or no cost is involved in the provision of the "goods" for sale, and those who have been trafficked are made to pay back any money that has been spent on everyday expenses such as food.

It is often said that, despite the fact that slavery has been outlawed, there are more slaves in the world today than ever before. There are several reasons for this. International travel is now much easier. People can be moved with ease from one country to another, by land, sea, or air. The Internet makes the buying and selling of people much easier than before. Traffickers can trap potential victims by advertising jobs that do not actually exist, or lure them into thinking that working in the West would solve all their problems. Political decisions can aid and abet trafficking. For example, while the relaxed borders of the European Union have brought many benefits to millions of people, they have also made it much easier for people to be moved from country to country without detection.

Such high rewards mean that unscrupulous and greedy people will always be looking for people to work for little or no pay, and without regard for their safety or working conditions. Whatever the job, young healthy people are required. The elderly and infirm are therefore not at risk of being trafficked. Those most vulnerable are poor people who live in countries in which there are few, if any, mechanisms in place to protect them from exploitation. A family living in dire straits might think that a life in bonded labor is better than one in which they do not know where their next meal is coming from. Freedom becomes less important when survival is the main problem. Young people who are living without parental supervision are often especially at risk. This is very prevalent in areas such as Eastern Europe where there is little or no hope of employment. Traffickers target impressionable young people whose parents have died or gone abroad to work, promising them Western lifestyles with plenty of money and good job prospects. Their victims dream of wealth and material goods and are easy prey for those who persuade them that this is possible. Often, they are young girls in their early teens who may have poor education and come from difficult family backgrounds. They are "groomed" by men who tell them that they are special and beautiful, and who trick them into thinking that they are in love with them. Young men are susceptible to false promises of good jobs abroad, but they then find that they are being exploited as slaves, or are so poorly paid that they will never be able to leave. It is also common for children to be forced to work as beggars, even by their own families.

Poverty is not the only issue, however. Poor education is also an important feature. Better-educated people are less likely to become slaves. The more they know and understand the risks, and the tactics used by traffickers, the more they will be able to protect themselves. People who are illiterate are often especially vulnerable. Traffickers prey on them by asking them to sign fake employment contracts. In countries like Indonesia, for example, many people are so desperate to find work that they will even leave by boat without any documentation at all. Different methods of coercion work in different cultures. For example, many women from African countries come to Europe knowing they will be working in prostitution, but believing that they are under a voodoo curse that will affect their families if they try to escape.

Racism can also be a factor. In some parts of Africa, for example, black people are easy prey for Arabs, while some tribes regard others as inferior and good sources of slaves. Other factors such as political instability and civil unrest can be a seedbed for human trafficking. In circumstances such as these, children are made to train as soldiers and women forced to provide sexual services for the military. It is known too that natural disasters such as flooding and earthquake can make desperate people vulnerable to those who are out to exploit others. All of these factors are aggravated by corruption. Where corruption is the norm, officials are more likely to turn a blind eye to human trafficking if they are offered bribes or included in a share of the profits.

In some areas, ideological belief systems can help to perpetuate slavery. In India, the caste system, with its view that certain groups of people are inferior to and of less value than others, helps perpetuate the existence of bonded labor. Kevin Bales reports these words of a slaveholder in India:

> Of course I have bonded laborers. I am a landlord. I keep them and their families, and they work for me. When they aren't in the fields, I have them doing the household work: Washing clothes, cooking, cleaning, making repairs, everything. After all, they are from the Kol caste; that's what they do, work for Vasyas [people of a higher caste] like me. I give them food and a little land to work. They've also borrowed money, so I have to make sure that they stay on my land till it is paid back. I don't care how old they get—you can't just give money away.[2]

These words give us an insight into how people can come to believe that slavery is inevitable. This man clearly thinks that what he is doing is natural and right: his workers belong to an inferior caste. By the same token, his slaves are likely to accept whatever happens to them as their fate.

---

2. Bales, *Understanding Global Slavery*, 33.

In religions such as Hinduism, which teach that suffering may have to be accepted as a consequence of misdeeds committed in previous lives, people are more likely to accept their lot and less likely to work against injustice. The same applies to sex trafficking. Wherever there is a view that women are inferior to men, there is a greater likelihood that women will be exploited in prostitution, and treated as objects rather than human beings in their own right.

Consequences of Trafficking

The suffering caused by human trafficking is immense. Families are split apart. Victims are beaten, tortured, raped. They have their property stolen, and even their personal identity, for example, if their personal papers are taken from them. They become non-persons. Slavery also has an effect on the psyche. If, like Mende Nazer, you are never called by your name, this does something to your sense of self. Victims lose hope; they can come to believe that there is no reason to live. They are separated from their families. They are deprived of education. Many die in captivity, or are discarded when they become ill or are no longer considered useful. Many attempt suicide.

The psychological damage caused by enslavement runs deep. Even if victims have not been subjected to physical or sexual abuse, they can come to believe that freedom is beyond their reach, or even come to fear the thought of it. They may fear the unknown, especially if, as in the case of bonded labor, their families have been enslaved over several generations. Some are born into slavery and know of no other way of life or being. The prospect of having to fend for oneself can be daunting—even if there is no physical reason why they cannot leave, it may seem easier to stay where they are. Many find it difficult to feed themselves and their families, whereas food was always assured before. How are they to pay medical bills and funeral costs?

The suffering inflicted by slavery does not necessarily end when someone is released from captivity. Individuals who have been brutalized and treated as commodities, as if they have no feelings, rights, or identity, can take some time to come to full realization of their true worth as persons, to believe in themselves once more, to get used to the idea that they are free. They may grieve the loss of friendships with others who were in the same situation as themselves. The so-called "Stockholm syndrome" may take effect—the enslaved person comes to have sympathy, loyalty, and even fondness for those who enslave them. In some ways captors and fellow slaves can become "family." On a more practical level, freedom may bring about homelessness and poverty. Those from a lower caste and in debt bondage may think it impossible to find alternative ways of finding work, let alone a way of thinking that they themselves are worth something. The security of debt bondage should not be underesti-mated: if the owner provides food, shelter, and work, however meagerly, seeking freedom can seem risky and even foolish.

Children who have been enslaved are unlikely to have received an education. Many cannot read and write, and therefore are unlikely to be able to find employment. They are accustomed only to working un-der certain situations of coercion and will not know how to take the initiative, how to think for themselves. In fact, removing a person from the situation of slavery can be highly traumatic, and this applies no matter what the work might have been—the one job she thought she could do is taken away. There is very little support in place for trafficked people who have been freed, but they need housing, jobs, and after-care. They may find themselves infected with TB or sexually transmitted diseases. They have many needs, and for some, the freedom is simply too much. They return to a situation of slavery because it feels easier. If freedom proves difficult, it can be easy for victims to slip into the old way of being. The old ways can be very attractive and provide security (psychological and material), despite the obvious hardships and dangers.

In particular, those who have been forced to work as prostitutes often discover that finding alternative employment is very difficult indeed. In many cultures, people who work as prostitutes are stigmatized and will be refused a job in any other industry. Their work-history is tarnished—it has a gap that cannot be filled. In his book, *The Natashas*, Victor Malarek tells the story of Tanya, who was trafficked from Ukraine to Abu Dhabi, where she thought she would be working as a maid, earning up to $4000 a month.

> But when she arrived in Abu Dhabi she was taken to a brothel where a pimp told her that he had bought her for $7000. From that moment on she was to work as a prostitute until she paid off her so-called debt. After three months of captivity, Tanya managed to escape. She bolted to a nearby police station and recounted her tale. Incredibly, she was charged with prostitution and sentenced to three years in a desert prison. In 2001, psychologically crushed and ashamed, Tanya was released. Branded as a prostitute by the Muslim nation, she was summarily deported back to her native Ukraine.[3]

Many women suffer rejection after having escaped from sex trafficking, even if their experiences are not as extreme as being sent to prison. It is not uncommon for women to be shunned by their families, and even not to be allowed to return to their home churches, when it becomes known that they have been working in prostitution. Often, people in this situation find that returning to the sex trade is their only option, for they know little else.

Many survivors of slavery suffer from post-traumatic stress disorder (PTSD). They suffer from nightmares, panic attacks, and flashbacks to the painful experiences they have endured. Those who have been repeatedly raped and beaten while in captivity suffer high instances of PTSD. The psychological effects for child soldiers are profound. They may be crippled by guilt because they have killed people, or by fear at the memory of the cruelty and control of their captors. The emotional effects of sex trafficking

---

3. Malarek, *The Natashas*, 12.

on victims are also severe. As well as PTSD, they may suffer from depression, anxiety, internal injuries, and infections (including HIV). Women may have had abortions and unwanted pregnancies. These findings do not give adequate expression to the sense of shame, anger, and grief that many feel. They may feel guilty, even though they were coerced and exploited, believing themselves to be worthless. They may find it difficult to build up relationship with others, not only unable to trust others, but themselves. Many feel guilt that they did not see through their traffickers and that they walked into their traps.

Conclusion

Human trafficking causes untold suffering throughout the world today. Mende Nazer was one of the lucky ones—she managed to escape. And we should be profoundly grateful to her for her courage in telling her story. However, many others do not escape, and still others are too traumatized and too ashamed to tell their stories. Some estimate that as many as 27 million people are enslaved today, and as we have seen, the causes are complex. Moreover, human trafficking continually proves very difficult to counteract. No sooner do police develop ways to respond than traffickers change their methods and approaches, in order to keep their lucrative business going. In the face of such evil, there is surely a need for Christians to be involved and to respond at all levels. If we believe in a loving God who demands that Christians make it their business to respond to the suffering in God's world, then we clearly have a responsibility to be informed of what is going on and to think carefully about how we respond to the complex issues. If we believe that Christ's love to the world is extended through his church, then we cannot stand idly by and allow millions to be exploited in this way.

But what can we do? As Christians, our first port of call is to turn to our Scriptures, the Bible. It not only gives us the theological basis for working against human trafficking, it also gives us insights into how the people of God can go about the task. However, we also have to find a way to listen to the Scriptures in our current situation, for as we have seen, there are many passages that uphold and support slavery, accepting it as a normal part of life. In the next chapter, we will try to learn some lessons from those who lived through the abolitionist campaign of the eighteenth and nineteenth centuries. What part did the Bible play in the debates, and how was it that so many Christians came to believe that slavery was contrary to

God's will? As we shall see, the relationship of the Bible to an anti-slavery viewpoint was far from straightforward, and there was a battle to be won before people were able to see things more clearly. We will now look at this debate and try to discover how it was that the abolitionists managed to work towards anti-slavery while at the same time believing that the Bible not only supported their cause, but gave them the courage and reason to pursue it.

 Questions for discussion.

1.   From a Christian point of view, what is wrong with slavery? What is wrong with the idea that one person may be the property of another?

2.   Do you think Christians should work against slavery? If so why, and how should we go about it?

3.   In your view, what features of modern society perpetuate human trafficking?

4.   What might prevent Christians from becoming involved in anti-slavery work?

5.   What do you think are the main causes of modern-day slavery?

6.   Read Mende Nazer's book, *Slave*, or some other account of experiences of slavery listed in the further reading section. Which aspect of their stories affect you most, and why?

7.   In your group, watch a film such as *The Whistleblower*, *12 Years a Slave*, or *Amazing Grace*. What aspect of the story do you find most interesting and moving? Why?

3

READING THE BIBLE: LESSONS FROM HISTORY

Introduction

It should surely go without saying that Christians have a moral duty to work against the injustice and suffering of human trafficking. In fact, many people do wonderful work at a practical level. Many are involved in rescuing the victims and caring for them, while others work in the world of politics and campaigning. However, we have seen what a complex thing contemporary human trafficking is, and that many different factors contribute to it. It is vital that Christians, no matter what their involvement in anti-slavery work might be, are able to think through how the church should respond. We also need to have spiritual food to give us the strength to enable us to do the work. For both these things, it is natural that we start by looking to the Bible to help us.

However, as we have also observed, when it comes to thinking about slavery, the Bible seems to give very mixed messages. On the one hand, it tells us that Jesus Christ came to set the captives free, and that Christians should fight against injustice in whatever form it takes. On the other hand, it never tells us that slavery should be abolished, and it contains many verses that seem to support it. This raises some very important questions for us. What should we do with the verses that support slavery? Should we ignore them altogether, pretending that they are not there? How can the

Bible speak to us and guide us in our fight against human trafficking when large parts of it seem to accept it and even support it?

Fortunately, we are not the first Christians to be faced with this problem. Anti-slavery activists in the eighteenth and nineteenth centuries were confronted with the same difficulty. They saw the injustice and suffering of slavery and knew that it must be contrary to the will of God. It ran counter to everything they knew and understood of God's love through their reading of the Bible. At the same time, though, there were many other Christians who were able to support slavery on biblical grounds. Indeed, the Bible became a major battleground in the slavery debate as both sides used it to back up their argument. It was the abolitionist cause that won the day, of course, but how did that come about? How was the "problem" of the Bible and slavery overcome?

In this chapter I shall tell the story of that debate, and the role of the Bible in it, for we can learn a great deal from it about how the Bible can speak to anti-trafficking work today. We shall see that the problem with regard to slavery and the Bible was not so much the Bible itself as the way it was understood and used by many who were involved. First though, it may be helpful to remind ourselves of how it came about that slavery was abolished in the nineteenth century.

A Brief Outline of the Abolitionist Story

Today, we have become so accustomed to the idea that slavery is morally wrong that we tend to forget that it was only just over two hundred years ago that governments began to think about trying to abolish it. The fact is that for most of human history, the majority of people, including Christians, thought it quite natural that some people should be masters and others slaves. Before the 1600s, few voices were raised against slavery. Some brave but isolated Christians did question the practice. The vast majority of Christians, however, considered slavery to be the norm. Around the 1680s, however, things began to change. Some American Quakers began to realize that owning slaves was incompatible with some of their dearly held principles—freedom, equality, and non-violence. Their ideas began to spread throughout America and across the Atlantic via the writings of Anthony Benezet and John Woolman. Gradually too, campaigners began draw to people's attention to the vast scale of the injustice and suffering involved in the slave trade. In Britain, two men—Thomas Clarkson and

Granville Sharp—made it their business to change things. They travelled throughout the land to inform people of the injustice of the slave trade, telling them about the suffering endured by those who were incarcerated on slave ships and taken against their will to work on cotton and sugar plantations. The Clapham Sect—a group of Christians led by the MP William Wilberforce—was instrumental in the introduction of the Abolition of the Slave Trade Act in 1807. In America, as Quaker ideas spread, many people, particularly in the Northern states, came to believe that slavery was unjust. For the Southern slaveholders, this was an attack on their way of life, and they worked hard to protect it. In 1850, the Fugitive State Law was passed, which decreed that runaway slaves to the North should be returned to their Southern owners. However, public opinion had changed to such an extent that many refused to go along with it. Not long after this, civil war broke out between the North and the South, at the cost of many lives. The North won. On 1st January 1863 the Emancipation Declaration came into effect, and in 1865, the 13th Amendment to the Constitution banned slavery altogether. What part did the Bible play in all this?

The Argument against Slavery Based on the Bible

The Quaker movement, which began in Britain in the seventeenth century, had at its core the belief that all people were created equal by God and had the right to be free. The Quakers were ostracized and punished for their views, and many went to America, believing that there they could live in religious freedom. Gradually however, they began to realize that the slaves who worked in the plantations and as domestic servants were hardly treated as free and equal, and many were subject to cruelty and violence. It took some time before the Quaker movement as a whole accepted anti-slavery views, not least because many of its leading members were themselves slave-owners. Nevertheless, the first recorded protest against slavery in North America, written in 1688, comes from the Germantown, Pennsylvania congregation of Mennonite Quakers who wrote to their monthly meeting:

> There is a saying, that we should do to all men like as we will be done ourselves; making no difference of what generation, descent or color they are.[1]

1. Reprinted in Morgan, *Slavery in America*, 370.

The saying, of course, was the "Golden Rule"—"in everything do to others as you would have them do to you" (Matt 7:12). Slaveholders would not want to be slaves themselves, so why should they be able to enslave others? Clearly, slave-holding was against Jesus' teaching as enshrined in the law of love.

The ideas spread to the United Kingdom, forcing Christians there to think again about their beliefs about slavery. In 1783, at their London Yearly Meeting, Quakers issued what they called a "publick testimony" against the slave trade. They quoted Jeremiah 22:13, warning that God would punish those who practiced slavery.

> Woe unto him, that buildeth his house by unrighteousness, and his chambers by wrong; that useth his neighbour's service without wages and giveth him not for his work.²

Anthony Benezet, in a very influential work entitled *A Caution to Great Britain*, emphasized equality between black and white people, and did so by referring to the creation story in Genesis.

> God gave to man dominion over the fish of the sea, and over the fowls of the air, and over the cattle, but imposed no involuntary subjection of one man to another.³

Arguments like these led people to realize that slavery was irreconcilable with biblical teaching about God's love and justice. Increasingly, clergy began to preach against slavery, telling their congregations that God would punish those involved. John Wesley, for example, in his "Thoughts Upon Slavery" (1774), told slaveholders that they would be subject to God's wrath on the day of judgment, when

> it shall be more tolerable for Sodom and Gomorrah than for you.
> The blood of thy brother crieth out against thee from the earth.
> Africans are creatures of God, for whom Christ died.⁴

In addition to drawing on the story of Sodom and Gomorrah, Wesley was alluding to the narrative in Genesis 4 in which Cain murders his brother Abel, a sin that cannot be hidden from God. Wesley used the biblical reference to make the point that slavery is murderous and cruel. Not

---

2. Dilwyn and Lloyd, *The Case of our Fellow-Creatures*, 15.

3. Benezet *A Caution to Great Britain*, 22.

4. Wesley, *Thoughts upon Slavery*, 25.

only that, it is wholly contrary to the teaching that Christ died for all men and women, not just for white people.

Throughout the anti-slavery campaign, many preachers drew on Scripture to make similar points. However, the most persuasive biblical text for most ordinary people was the one that the Quakers had first given— slavery was simply against the law of love. The Bible taught that Christians should love their neighbors. They were to show mercy and help the poor. Where did slavery fit in with these teachings? Increasingly, Christians on both sides of the Atlantic found the existence of slavery impossible to justify.

The Argument for Slavery Based on the Bible

At the same time, however, supporters of slavery also referred to Scripture to support their cause. Indeed, the more the anti-slavery campaigners referred to the Bible, the more the pro-slavery lobby adopted the same tactics. They frequently pointed out that the Bible did not forbid slavery, and argued that it was part of God's plan. One common argument was that the Bible had prophesied that black people would be enslaved. This claim was made on the basis of the story in Genesis 9, in which Noah becomes drunk and is discovered by his son Ham. Noah angrily puts a curse on Ham's descendants, saying, "Cursed be Canaan: lowest of slaves shall he be to his brothers" (Gen 9:10). In the commonly held view of the time, Canaan was understood to refer to Africa, and if that was the case then African people must be under a curse. This not only provided an explanation as to why black people should be considered inferior to white people, it also allowed the pro-slavery campaigners to argue that it was written in Scripture that they would be slaves.

Another argument was that slaveholders were following the example of Abraham and the patriarchs, and so were being obedient to biblical principles. According to Genesis 20:14, for example, the fact that Abraham had many male and female servants demonstrated that God's blessing was on him and his family. The same could be said for Jacob, who, when he became rich, also had many slaves (Gen 30:43). Thus, Southern slaveholders attributed their prosperity to the fact that they were following biblical principles for an orderly society, and maintained that God's will should not be challenged. Some believed that the black slave trade was actually commanded by God, and in support of this they cited Leviticus 25:44–45:

Biblical slave — owner.

> As for the male and female slaves whom you may have, it is from
> the nations around you that you may acquire male and female
> slaves. You may also acquire them from the aliens residing with
> you, and from their families that are with you, who have been born
> in your land; and they may be your property.

On this basis, one clergyman by the name of Rev. Fred Ross, in a book
entitled *Slavery Ordained of God*, argued that it was God's will that slaves
should be bought from foreign countries. Indeed, many argued that by
obeying this commandment, American Christians were helping to rescue
black people from their pagan background, and giving them the chance of
hearing the gospel. Slavery was thus a way to help save the souls of those
from a race that was under the "curse of Ham." Pro-slavery campaigners
also found support for their cause in the New Testament. Primarily, they
noted that neither Jesus nor Paul said that slavery should be stopped. In
fact, Paul himself had instructed Philemon to take back his runaway slave,
Onesimus. Other passages were also very important to the proslavery

cause. In 1 Timothy, for example, there is a direct instruction that makes it clear that slaves are to obey their masters.

> Let all who are under the yoke of slavery regard their masters as worthy of all honor, so that the name of God and the teaching may not be blasphemed. Those who have believing masters must not be disrespectful to them on the ground that they are members of the church; rather they must serve them all the more, since those who benefit by their service are believers and beloved. (1 Tim 6:1–2)

Passages like these not only reassured slaveholders that they were acting in accordance with God's will, but also were very useful in encouraging obedience and discouraging rebellion amongst their slaves. Scripture was considered an important part of slaves' education. Slaves were repeatedly reminded that Scripture taught that they should be obedient to their masters. An example of this is a catechism that slaves were taught to recite, written by Elias Neau for the Anglican Society for the Propagation of the Gospel in Foreign Parts in 1704.[5]

5. Quoted in Callahan, *The Talking Book*, 31–32.

> Who gave you a master and a mistress?
>
> God gave them to me.
>
> Who says that you must obey them?
>
> God says that I must.
>
> What book tells you these things?
>
> The Bible.

The catechism was designed to instill in the slaves that to disobey commandments like these would be to disobey God himself. Consequently, they should behave well and not question their masters or their lack of freedom.

There was therefore ample scriptural evidence on which slaveholders could draw to defend their practices. Some arguments, such as the one based on the "curse of Ham," were clearly contrived, and anti-slavery theologians could easily point out their flaws. However, others, like the commands to slaves to obey their masters, seemed much harder to argue against. The result was that many sincere Christians were convinced that God's word supported slavery, and that it ought to be obeyed.

Both sides then, could cite the Bible in support of their stance. The abolitionists, on the one hand, thought that the pro-slavers were deliberately ignoring a much higher law—the law of love—and were doing so in order to perpetuate their own way of life, without concern for justice and the need to relieve suffering. The pro-slavers, believing that the Bible gave them direct instruction, considered that the abolitionists were being dishonest in their reading—deliberately ignoring the plain meaning of the text, and devaluing Scripture into the bargain.

The Princetonians

There can be no doubt that for many slaveholders the Bible was merely a tool to be used to support their way of life. It was convenient to cite the Bible to prop up their argument and to use it as a weapon against their abolitionist enemies. However, a great many people genuinely wanted to be obedient to God and believed that the way to do so was to obey the instructions contained in the Bible. For such Christians it was important to follow the plain meaning of the text and do what it said. So, if the Bible said that slaves were to obey their masters, then they should do so. For some Christians, however, this approach to Scripture created something of a dilemma. They felt deeply uneasy about slavery, but at the same time wanted to ensure that biblical authority was not undermined. Thus, they found themselves in a rather difficult position. One famous example of this is Charles Hodge, who was principal of Princeton Seminary in New Jersey, and whose views were published in *The Biblical Repertory and Princeton Review*, a widely read and highly influential journal. Hodge himself believed that slavery was not in line with God's plan. However, since the Bible did not contain a commandment against slavery, he could not bring himself to support the abolitionist cause. In fact, he thought that abolitionism was a sin. God would bring about the ending of slavery in his own time, but human beings should not work to bring it to an end—because there was no biblical instruction to do so.

The Princeton school of interpretation was influenced by contemporary philosophical and scientific ideas. From philosophy (in particular, Scottish "common sense" philosophy) they learned the importance of "sense experience" and physical evidence, as the basis for knowledge. Reason should replace superstition. At the same time, scientists such as Newton were learning to observe, measure, and document the natural world. In the same way, the Princetonian scholars believed, it was the job of the theologian to describe truth, and the Bible contained all the data necessary for this task. Problems like that of slavery had to be seen in the light of that data. Was it God's will to abolish slavery? Hodge could find no evidence in Scripture to say so. Since there was no direct command to abolish slavery to be found in the Bible, he had to conclude that abolitionism must be contrary to God's will. Thus, despite the fact that Hodge did not support slavery himself, his approach to the Bible meant that he unintentionally propped up the pro-slavers' cause, and indirectly contributed to the prolonging of injustice and suffering.

Impasse

The argument on the basis of the Bible came to something of an impasse, and it comes as no surprise to learn that some prominent anti-slavery campaigners decided to disregard the Bible altogether, believing that it was hindering the abolitionist cause. Meanwhile, however, some important developments were taking place that would ensure that the abolitionists won the day. First, campaigners produced more evidence of the injustice and suffering endured by slaves themselves. In the UK, the public was outraged by the case of the slave ship Zong, in which a sea captain threw many slaves overboard in order to claim insurance. Then, in 1791, a document named *An Abstract of the Evidence* was produced containing deeply shocking evidence of the ill-treatment of slaves by military officers, sea captains, and doctors. In America in 1839, Theodore D. Weld produced a document called *Slavery as It Is: Testimony of a Thousand Witnesses*, which contained reports of torture and harsh punishments of slaves. It sold 22,000 copies within four months of its publication, and its evidence persuaded many to join the campaign.

Secondly, some former slaves began to write of their experiences and to publish their accounts. Writers such as Frederick Douglass drew attention to the hypocrisy of slaveholders who claimed to be Christian. From experience he was able to speak of the sufferings slavery caused and he could see that Christian doctrine and slavery were incompatible. Black people, as well as whites, were made in the image of God.

> The slave is a man, "the image of God," but a "little lower than the angels"; possessing a soul, eternal and indestructible; capable of endless happiness, or immeasurable woe. . . . The first work of slavery is to mar and deface those characteristics of its victims which distinguish men from things and persons from property.[6]

Similarly, Phillis Wheatley, a slave who became the first black woman to publish poetry in the United States, reminded Christians of God's love for all people

> That there's a God, that there's a *Savior* too:
> Once I redemption neither sought nor knew.
> Some view our sable race with scornful eye,
> "Their color is a diabolic die."
> Remember, Christians, Negroes, black as Cain,
> May be refin'd, and join the angelic train.[7]

Writers like these brought to the attention of white readers that black people were not the ignorant, uncultured people they had taken them for. They could read the Bible, and interpret for themselves. They could write spirituals such as "Let my People Go" and "Go Down Moses," singing of a God who redeems his people from slavery, and be sustained and inspired

---

6. See Ruston, *Human Rights and the Image of God*, 269.

7. Quoted in Carretta, *Unchained Voices*, 62.

READING THE BIBLE: LESSONS FROM HISTORY   33

by the message of love and redemption in Jesus Christ, who shared their sufferings.

Third, in 1852 a novel was published that was to become the most influential writing of the American abolitionist campaign. Harriet Beecher Stowe's *Uncle Tom's Cabin* helped people to see slaves as human beings, and made their terrible suffering its central theme. But Stowe was not only a fine storyteller, she also well understood that different views of the Bible were crucial in the slavery debate. At one point in the novel, when Uncle Tom is being taken by boat to another owner, we overhear this conversation between two passengers. One is a minister, who says,

> It's undoubtedly the intention of Providence that the African race should be servants—kept in low condition. "Cursed be Canaan; a servant of servants shall he be," the Scripture says.

However, his conversation partner sees that the law of love is much more important than this argument.

> "'All things whatsoever ye would that men do unto you, do you even so unto them.' I suppose," he added, "that is Scripture, as much as cursed be Canaan."[8]

Stowe makes it clear that the minister has lost any sense of compassion and has forgotten the true meaning of the gospel. He is much more interested in being part of a "superior" race than he is in the love of Christ for all men demonstrated in Scripture.

Learning the Lessons

At the beginning of the abolitionist debate most people believed that the Bible permitted slavery. At the end of it most Christians believed that slavery ought to be stopped on the basis of the "law of love." The story of the use of the Bible in the American abolitionist debate reveals that there was a battle, not merely between those who supported slavery and those who did not, but also between different ways of understanding the Bible. Broadly speaking, there were two different approaches to Scripture. For one group, the Bible was regarded as a book of moral prescription and data. As we have seen, not everyone who took this view of the Bible was in favor of slavery, but many people, including influential theologians and clergy, felt

8. Stowe, *Uncle Tom's Cabin*, 115–16.

they could not support abolitionism because it was not prescribed in Scripture. For ordinary readers, this way of reading the Bible was instinctive and natural—it took the text at face value and provided direct instruction and teaching. For the influential scholars of the Princeton school, this approach was shaped and endorsed by Enlightenment philosophy, which underlined the importance of finding evidence and proof in the quest for scientific data. The task of biblical scholarship was to find the original and universally valid meaning. Unfortunately, however, this approach tended to give a blinkered perspective in which the need for personal obedience to biblical instruction could take precedence over the call to respond to suffering and injustice.

The other, ultimately successful, approach saw a much bigger picture. The anti-slavery campaigners, the Quakers and the slaves themselves, took the view that the Bible is not primarily a book of data and moral prescription, but a story—the story of God's intervention in history. The main message of that story was of God's great love for the world demonstrated in the life of Jesus Christ. But this great love of God required a response from believers, and this response was encapsulated in the Golden Rule. They were to treat other people in the way they would want to be treated themselves. With this as their starting point, slavery had to be seen as unacceptable. Since they would not want to be the slave of another, slavery had to be incompatible with the law of love, which as Scripture itself said, summed up the law and the prophets. There could be no choice but to do something about it.

The abolitionists' approach to the Bible reminds us that the story of Jesus Christ's redeeming death and resurrection points to liberation as a central Christian value. Redemption is offered to all, and it is this that provides us with the theological basis for our response to modern-day slavery. As we look to the Bible to teach us more for our current struggle against slavery, we shall therefore follow their example, understanding everything we read in the Bible in the light of the central truth that Jesus Christ has come as the redeeming God who sets the captives free.

The story of the Bible in the abolitionist debate has other lessons to teach us. It reminds us of the temptation that can beset all who want the Bible to be authoritative in their lives—that is the temptation to reduce it to nothing more than an instruction manual. When this happens, we not only rob the Scriptures of their great richness and depth, we also run the risk of becoming preoccupied with our own moral "rightness." Reading the Bible serves only to reassure us that we are right and that those who disagree with us are wrong, and disobeying God. But this way of reading ultimately is self-defeating and destructive—as Paul says, "the letter kills but the Spirit gives life" (2 Cor 3:6). Those who wanted to use the Bible merely as a book of "scientific data" or moral prescription fell into the trap of interpreting it in a way that "killed" rather than gave life. Against even their better instincts, they ultimately contributed to the prolonging of suffering and injustice, rather than being driven by compassion for others born out of a love for God.

The story of the Bible in the abolitionist campaign also reminds us that we need to be aware of our own presuppositions and agendas as we come to the text. We have a tendency to see in Scripture what we want to see. During the time of the abolitionist debate it was fashionable to think that we could be as objective in our reading of the Bible as say, a scientist could be when he was documenting what he saw in the natural world. Today, however, we are much more aware that when we read, we start with certain presuppositions that are informed by our cultures, our political or religious opinions, and our own personal agendas. The pro-slavers' agenda was to maintain their way of life, and so they read in the Bible what would support their cause. The antislavery advocates and the slaves themselves wanted the ending of slavery and saw in its pages the moral imperative of ending it, even though this was never directly stated. So, the first step in our biblical interpretation is an honest admission that we are as much products of our times as the abolitionists were in theirs. We must also try to discern our motivations as we read the Bible, for as we have seen, it is possible to use the Bible for our own purposes rather than to further God's kingdom. It may be that we are using the Bible to confirm our own prejudices, or to maintain our own positions of power. The abolitionist story teaches us that we must be as honest as possible with ourselves and be open to different points of view, to learn from others, and to have our "blind spots" challenged.

With these lessons in mind, then, we will now turn to the Bible itself. At the outset we are declaring that we take an anti-slavery stance. We believe that human trafficking is contrary to God's will. Like the abolitionists of the eighteenth and nineteenth centuries, we approach the text in the knowledge that millions of people are suffering because they or members of their families are enslaved, and with the desire to see peoples' lives changed. We know too that the biblical worldview differs from our own with regard to slavery, but that it also contains an overarching message of love and redemption—a message that we believe still to be powerful in our world today. In the light of this knowledge, we ask the question: what does the Bible say about contemporary human trafficking?

Questions for discussion.

1. Think about your own approach to Scripture. What are you looking for when you read the Bible?

2. The Bible contains sixty-six books, and many stories, poems, and laws. What do you think the overall message of Scripture is?

3. What do you understand by the phrase "the Spirit gives life but the letter kills"?

4. From your own experience, can you think of any examples in which you believe the law of love was eclipsed by a need to adhere to rules or customs?

5. Why did the law of love triumph in the case of the slavery debate?

6. What can we learn from the abolitionists' use of the Bible for today's anti-slavery work?

7. The Princeton scholars were very much influenced by current ideas in philosophy and science, and these had a significant effect on how they read the Bible. What ideas and assumptions might influence your own reading of the Bible today?

8. During the abolitionist debate, each group looked to the Bible to support their own agenda or cause. Can you think of any occasions in which you have heard a group or individual refer to the Bible to support their own political or personal purposes? How did they do this? Was it for a good or a bad purpose? How did people respond?

4

SLAVERY IN THE OLD TESTAMENT

Introduction

IN THIS CHAPTER WE will focus on passages that deal with slavery in the Old Testament. We will begin with the laws that were so important to the pro-slavers, who used them to uphold their cause. They saw them as support for their slave-holding activities and even as evidence that slavery was commanded by God. Can they have anything to say to us at all, or do we have to discard them as useless for our contemporary lives? We need to be careful, however, not to become preoccupied with law, and remember that there is much, much more to the Old Testament than this. The theme of slavery is prominent in many stories, not least the Exodus narrative, in which Moses leads the people of Israel out of slavery in Egypt. It is also mentioned in wisdom literature and some prophetic books. What do these passages have to say to us about a Christian response to human trafficking?

The Laws Regarding Slavery

Slavery was a fact of life in the Old Testament world. In the earliest stories, we read that Abraham had both male and female slaves (Gen 12:16), and that Isaac's slaves dug wells for water when he settled in the valley of Gerar (Gen 26:19). In Genesis 30:43, it is reported that Jacob became "exceedingly prosperous" and that he had camels and donkeys, large flocks of sheep, and male and female slaves. A couple of stories bear witness to the common practice of female slaves being used to bear children on behalf of their childless owners—what we would call today surrogate motherhood. The female slave involved had no rights or say in the matter. For example, Hagar bears a son (Ishmael) for Abraham when Sarah cannot conceive, and great animosity arises between the two women. In the end, though, it is Hagar who has to go, and Sarah maintains her place as the matriarch of Israel. In Genesis 30, Rachel's slave Bilhah bears two sons by Jacob: Dan and Naphthali. Another story in which slavery features prominently is the story of Jacob's son, Joseph. Today, we would say that Joseph was a victim of human trafficking. He was sold by his brothers to the Ishmaelites, who then sold him on to Egyptians, and he then became a slave in the house of Potiphar.

However, slavery was not only a fact of life, it was also highly significant for the ancient Hebrews, for they themselves were held in captivity in Egypt. Like many slaves today, they were forced to work in the construction industry. They had to make bricks, were badly treated, and were accused of laziness when they asked to hold their own festivals and religious ceremonies (Exod 5:17). Eventually, of course, Moses led them out of Egypt and into freedom, and their escape from captivity was to be the story that gave them their identity—no matter what happened to them, they should always remember that they were the people whom God had set free.

However, although the Hebrews suffered greatly while they were in Egypt it would never have occurred to them to consider abolishing slavery, or even to think that there was anything wrong with it. For, in common with all the other nations around them, the ancient Hebrews thought it quite normal and acceptable to keep slaves. So it was that, after their release from forced labor, the Israelites had slaves of their own.

As they adjusted to their new freedom, and began to develop as a nation, the Israelites began to devise legislation in order to ensure the smooth running of society. As in any society, in addition to laws designed to ensure that their religious life and practices functioned well, regulations had to be put in place to ensure that personal property was protected, that violence was discouraged, and that families were able to live and work in peace. These laws are preserved for us in three collections in the Old Testament, in Exodus, Deuteronomy, and Leviticus, and some deal specifically with how slaves should be treated.

There were two main groups of slaves. The first, and probably the larger group, was made up of chattel slaves, who were regarded as the personal property of their masters. Chattel slaves were foreigners, generally brought back as prisoners of war and made to work in domestic and agricultural work. In fact, in Leviticus 25:44–46, express permission is given to buy slaves from the surrounding countries, or foreigners living in the land.

When the owner of chattel slaves died, these slaves were to be considered property to be passed on to their children.

The second kind of slavery in ancient Israel was debt-bondage. Owning foreign slaves was to be thought quite normal, but the idea that Israelites themselves should be slaves was frowned upon, and efforts were made to ensure that this happened as little as possible. Human trafficking of fellow Israelites was expressly forbidden (Deut 24:7), and the penalty for those caught was death. There was a direct instruction that Hebrews were not to be sold to non-Israelites (Lev 25:42), and if any Hebrews were in such dire straits that they sold themselves as slaves to foreigners, their families were expected to buy them back (Lev 25:47–52). However, some Israelites do seem to have become so poor that they felt that they had no alternative but to become slaves of fellow Hebrews in order for their families to survive. Thus, in ways perhaps similar to the debt-bondage in which so many construction and mine workers throughout the world find themselves today, some sold themselves and their families into the ownership of another, who would give them food, shelter, and clothing in return for work.

While it was recognized that this may be the only way that a poor Israelite could survive, debt bondage of this sort was frowned upon, and measures were taken to protect those who found themselves in this unfortunate situation. Perhaps knowing that those in debt-bondage were vulnerable to extortion—for example, that additions to the original debt could be made to the extent that it was impossible for the slave to pay it back—laws were made to try to ensure that the period of servitude did not last indefinitely. In Exodus 21 and Deuteronomy 15:12, there are instructions that no Hebrew was to be kept in debt-bondage for more than seven years, and when they were set free they were to be given provisions to help them to begin this new phase in their lives. In Leviticus 25:39–40, the instructions are slightly different. Those in debt bondage were to be treated as hired servants rather than slaves and were to be released from debt bondage in the year of Jubilee (Lev 25:40).

The lawmakers did recognize, however, that sometimes a good relationship could develop between master and slave and that it might be beneficial to both to continue with the arrangement. Some debt slaves might have felt a special loyalty to their masters, or thought that their current situation of slavery was the best option for them and their families. In such cases, it was important to make the agreement public knowledge and to ensure that no misunderstandings arose. So, a special ceremony was to take place in which the servant had his ear pierced to indicate that he had opted to remain the slave of his master (Exod 21:5–6; Deut 15:16–17). Neverthe-less, the community leaders would have preferred that Israelites were never in a situation in which enslavement seemed to be a good option in the first place. To this end, they tried to protect people from becoming destitute. For example, laws were devised to ensure that no interest should be charged against a loan (Lev 25:35–38), and against dishonest financial transactions (Deut 24:7; 25:13–16; Lev 19:35–37). In other words, those in positions of power were not to take advantage of the poor or vulnerable.

Of course, how slaves were treated depended on the individual owner. Some would look after their slaves well, while others could be cruel or harsh. The Hebrew lawmakers were well aware of these dangers, and the le-gal collections contain examples of efforts to curb the possibility of cruelty and abuse. For example, if a master punished one of his slaves so severely that the slave died, the master himself was to be punished (Exod 21:20). If a slave was injured as the result of a punishment then that slave could go free (Exod 21:26).

It is probable that these laws applied to both foreign chattel slaves and Hebrews in debt-bondage, but in general, there were clear differences between the two groups and how they were to be treated. For instance, according to Leviticus 25:39–40, people in debt-bondage (that is, Israelites) were to be treated as though they were hired servants rather than slaves. The release laws, whether they spoke of liberation for slaves every seven years or in the year of Jubilee, applied only to Hebrew debt-slaves. Foreign-ers who had been brought to Israel as chattel slaves, seem to have had no option of returning to their families, but had to adopt the way of life of their masters. This would, of course, have been a profoundly painful expe-rience for the slaves, and in Deuteronomy 21:10–14 there is some evidence that the lawmakers recognized this. Foreign slaves were often captured in war, and soldiers were allowed to capture foreign women in wartime and marry them, but these women are to be given time to grieve the loss of their homes and families. If the soldier later changed his mind, he was to let the woman go free. The purpose of this law was to give some dignity to the for-eign women, but even a law such as this would not take away the fact that the women were being treated very cruelly indeed, taken away from every-thing they knew and sexually exploited—forced to marry against their will. No matter how kindly individual masters may have treated them, foreign slaves were, to use Orlando Patterson's phrase, subject to "natal alienation," removed from all that they knew and robbed of their culture and identity.[1]

1. Patterson, *Slavery and Social Death,* 13.

It is important to note that Israel was not the only country to have slave laws of this sort. Other nations also made attempts to keep slavery under control and curtail excess cruelty and abuse. For example, an ancient Mesopotamian law collection known as the Babylonian Hammurabi Code contains laws that were intended to prescribe for the protection of slaves and punishment for runaways. What made the Hebrew laws different, however, was the thinking that underpinned them. The reasons for the legislation on slavery—the attempts to curtail cruelty and the laws for release of debt slaves—are theological, and they are reiterated throughout the law collections. First, the Hebrews considered themselves to be made in the image of God. There was therefore a belief in the inherent dignity of the human person. This belief is probably the basis for the instructions against excessive punishment, maiming, or mutilation (Exod 21:26–27).

Second, all Hebrews believed themselves to have been set free, by God himself, from debt bondage in Israel. YHWH had delivered them, and had made a covenant with them (e.g., Exod 20:2; Deut 7:6–11; 8:11–20).[2] The Hebrews were not to hold their own people in long-term debt bondage precisely because they had all been rescued by YHWH (Lev 25:39; Deut 15:12). Thus the Jubilee law in in Leviticus 25:39–43 states:

> If any who are dependent on you become so impoverished that they sell themselves to you, you shall not make them serve as slaves. They shall remain with you as hired or bound laborers. They shall serve with you until the year of the Jubilee. Then they and their children with them shall be free from your authority; they shall go back to their own family and return to their ancestral property. For they are my servants, whom I brought out of the land of Egypt; they shall not be sold as slaves are sold. You shall not rule over them with harshness, but shall fear your God.

The memory of the exodus also meant that Hebrews must treat foreigners who were resident and working as hired hands with humanity (Deut 24:15, 17). God had responded to the suffering of His people, so the Hebrews must behave like Him by treating foreigners well (Deut 24:18). Thus, slaves were to have the Sabbath rest and to observe festivals along with everyone else (Deut 5:14; 12:12; 16:11; Exod 20:10). When those in debt bondage were set free, they were to be given provisions for the start of the new phase of their lives, because the Hebrews had been given silver when they left Egypt (Deut 15:13–15).

---

2. The letters YHWH are the consonants of the Hebrew designation for God.

So we see that while the lawmakers and the early Israelites were similar to other nations, they viewed the world and their situation differently. That is, they looked at the world through the lens of their self-understanding as people who had been redeemed by God. It was this worldview that allowed them to consider enslavement of fellow Hebrews to be distasteful, and that also formed the basis of the idea that even foreigners ought to be treated as fellow human beings.

Stories of Slaves and Their Owners

Just as the laws reflect the fact that slavery was part of life, many Old Testament stories testify to the continuing belief that it was acceptable to consider another human being as personal property. However, in these stories there are subtle voices that question this view, and that urge us to think more deeply about our attitudes towards those whom society thinks worthless.

There is, for example, throughout the Old Testament, a recurring theme that those whom society discounts have a crucial role to play in God's plan. Slaves may be thought by most people to count for nothing, but they can be the voice of God. For example, in 2 Kings 5, Naaman, the commander of the king of Aram's army, suffers from leprosy. His wife's slave, a Hebrew girl who had been captured when the Aramaeans had raided Israel, suggests to her mistress that Naaman consult Elisha the prophet. When Elisha tells him to wash in the Jordan seven times, Namaan becomes angry, for he had expected that Elisha would come to see him and cure him on the spot. Naaman's servants urge him to do as Elisha suggests, however, and when he does as he has been instructed, he is cured. Thus, Naaman's servants are able to see the wisdom of the prophet in a way that the powerful Namaan cannot. Moreover, the slave-girl is astute, clever, and compassionate, even to those who have taken her from her home and robbed her of her freedom. A similar point is made in the story of Joseph. He is sold into slavery in Egypt, but becomes so successful that he is made the head of Potiphar's household. Joseph is shown to have more integrity than Potiphar's wife, who tries to seduce him and accuses him of rape when he resists her. He is also able to interpret dreams and Pharaoh recognizes that he has the "spirit of God" (Gen 41:37). And, of course, he shows mercy and forgiveness to his brothers (the ones who had sold him into slavery in the first place) when they need help.

These stories of Hebrews who become the slaves of foreigners have a powerful message. They show that people who are slaves, however society might view them, never lose their dignity as human beings. In fact, they may even be cleverer and more gifted than their owners. Both Naaman's wife's slave-girl and Joseph are used by God to further his purposes and show compassion to those who treat them unjustly.

This idea is not confined to Hebrew slaves, however. For example, in Genesis 24 we have the story of Abraham's servant. This servant is trustworthy and loyal, and he is also faithful to his master's God, despite being a foreigner himself. He prays for guidance, and so is able to secure Rebekah as Isaac's wife. Here again, someone who is considered to be a non-person by society (we are not told the servant's name) is used by God, and shown to be capable of great faith, wisdom, and discernment. The story shows that he is certainly not a non-person in God's eyes. Rather, he has great dignity and is very important for the continuation of the people of Israel.

Similarly, in Genesis 16, when relations sour between Hagar and Sarah, and Hagar runs away, an angel of the Lord comes to her and tells her that she will have a son whom she is to call Ishmael, meaning "God hears." Later, when she has been sent away by Abraham and has run out of water, God provides a well, ensuring that she and her son survive (Gen 21:8–20). The angel of the Lord addresses this slave girl, whom Abraham and Sarah refer to only as "slave," by *name*, and her son becomes a great nation in his own right.

Slavery in the Writings and Prophets

References to slaves are also found in the books of Ecclesiastes, Job, and Proverbs. These books are part of a group known as wisdom literature and they contain sayings and insights into life that have been collected over centuries. In Proverbs 19:10 we read: "It is not fitting for a fool to live in luxury—how much worse for a slave to rule over princes." This, along with a similar saying in 30:22, is really an observation that there is a need for everyone to recognize his or her place in society. We find much the same in Ecclesiastes 5:7: "I have seen slaves on horseback, while princes go on foot like slaves." In other words, rulers who allow their slaves to gain power over them are likely to find themselves losing their position of power, and becoming a laughingstock. These writers are, therefore, very much concerned with maintaining the status quo, for the wellbeing of everyone in society. However, this does not mean that slaves are to be ill-treated or considered as non-persons. Proverbs 17:2 notes that slaves can be wise, and can be great assets in family life, while Proverbs 30:10 warns that slaves need to be treated sensibly and with respect, for they could retaliate if they are handled badly. As Job says, slaves are human beings, created by God, and those who ill-treat their slaves will be called to account (Job 31:13–15).

The prophets are concerned for the poor and powerless. In particular, they protest against corruption and oppression (Jer 22:13–19; Mal 3:5), and they frequently remind the people that they themselves had been brought out of Egypt (Amos 2:10; 3:1; 9:7; Hos 13:4–6; Mic 6:2–8). In Jeremiah 34:12–16, we read that King Zedekiah made a covenant with the people of Jerusalem that they should release their Hebrew slaves. The people duly did so. However, they then changed their minds, and made those they had freed slaves again. Jeremiah intervenes, reminds them of the seven-year release commandment, and says that they will be punished severely for keeping God's people captive. Joel protests against human trafficking, including the selling of children in exchange for prostitutes and wine, and warns that similar things could happen to their own children (Joel 3:1–6). Amos also objects to oppression of the poor and human trafficking.

> Thus says the Lord: "For three transgressions of Israel, and for four, I will not revoke the punishment; because they sell the righteous for silver, and the needy for a pair of sandals, they who trample the head of the poor into the dust of the earth, and push the afflicted out of the way." (Amos 2:6–7)

However, since Israel is YHWH's redeemed people, whom he rescued from oppression, it is fundamentally contradictory for Israel to oppress the poor, and once again, dire punishment will come upon them if they do not change their practices.

We saw in the narratives the idea that God can work through those whom society rejects. This idea is developed fully in Isaiah, who speaks of a suffering servant or slave (the Hebrew word is the same for both) who, though he is despised and rejected himself, will restore justice to Israel and bring salvation to all people (Isa 42:1–4; 49:1–6; 50:4–9; 52:13–53:12). There will be a new exodus (Isa 43:16–21; 51:9–11) in which the slave will bring Israel, and indeed all nations, back to God. Throughout Isaiah 40–66 there is the idea that Israel must follow this example of the redeeming God and be an example to the nations, being merciful and just in their dealings with them.

Contemporary Application:
Discerning the Voice of Love and Redemption

At first sight, the Old Testament seems to give us mixed messages with regard to the morality of slavery. It is repeated over and again that the exodus story was key to how Israel understood herself, and from that we might expect that the idea of freedom and justice is central to all that Israel stood for. However, despite this, they continued the practice of keeping slaves. Furthermore, although there is evidence that some had doubts about slavery, these doubts seem only to have led to attempts to curtail it amongst their own people. It seems still to have been considered acceptable to kidnap foreigners and make them work as chattel slaves. In other words, there were double standards.

In order to help us make sense of this, it is helpful to think of the Old Testament as containing several strands of thinking. Its thirty-nine books include different voices from different points in history, and these voices bear witness to varying points of view. Today, we have to try to distinguish between these voices. Certain strands in the biblical literature reflect everyday life in ancient Israel, and from them we can glean some information as to how people lived their lives. For example, we have seen that Abraham and the patriarchs owned slaves, and that female slaves were used as surrogate mothers. Information of this sort reflects common assumptions and practices that were common within society, and enables us to learn who was considered to have power and honor, and who was considered to be of inferior status.

At the same time, we can also discern strands of tradition that question these assumptions and practices. These challenging voices are to be heard, for example, in the stories that show slaves as honorable, clever human beings used by God, or in Job's reflection that slaves are human beings too. They undermine, often subtly, the commonly held assumption that slaves are non-persons, and that it is acceptable to treat them as such. In particular, the story of the exodus questions such assumptions, for the idea of freedom and human dignity is at its very core. It is highly significant that this story is constantly reiterated as a reminder of who the Israelites were, where they had come from, and as a basis for their self-understanding and how to relate to others. It is repeated so often that it is clear that those who kept and collected the documents that became the Hebrew Scriptures saw it as providing the values that were to form the basis of the lives of the people of Israel. We might refer to this as the voice of love and redemption, or even the voice of God.

We hear this voice in the prophets who challenged the oppression of the poor, and against the corruption and greed that perpetuated poverty and debt-slavery. In their opinion, when Israel forgot its special relationship with the God who had redeemed them, corruption, greed, and injustice gained a foothold in public life, and it was the poor who suffered. In Isaiah's view, this pattern of thinking was so ingrained and harmful to society that one day, a redeemer would have to come to rescue the people from themselves and their sin. But contrary to expectation this redeemer would not embody the values that human beings had come to honor: status, wealth, and power. He would be a slave himself, and he would suffer and be rejected, but would ultimately redeem his people once more. Eventually people would realize that God's redemption applied not only to Israel, but to *all* the peoples of the world.

We also hear this voice in the law collections, for example, in the attempts to curtail the abuse of slaves, the provisions for slave-release, and in the laws that attempt to reduce corruption and oppression of the poor. It is perhaps particularly to be heard in Deuteronomy 23:15–16 in which fugitive slaves are to be given asylum, for no other country, so far as we know, had such a law. But what are we to make of the fact that the law collections seem to legislate for double standards—for most of these provisions apply only to Hebrew debt slaves and not to the foreign chattel slaves? How should we understand this?

Following their liberation from Egypt, the Israelites had to learn how to be free. After years of servitude, they found freedom hard to adjust to, and even at one point complained that they had been better off in captivity. There was a constant temptation to forget their allegiance to YHWH and to worship other gods. And as in any community, crimes such as theft and murder were bound to occur. So, they needed to set boundaries and lay down rules for the smoother running of society. As time passed and circumstances changed, some laws were revised, new ones introduced, and others discarded. In fact, several collections of laws have been preserved for us, each reflecting the attempts of lawmakers to create the kind of society they wanted at various times in Israel's history (e.g., Exod 21; Lev 25; Deut 15). Together, they give us glimpses of the development and change over centuries as the lawmakers decided how best to live life well. They were collated and preserved, according to Richard Bauckham, "to educate the people in the will of God for the whole of their life as his people, to create and develop the conscience of the community."[3] In other words, they are records of how people responded to human behavior in differing circumstances and the attempts to live out the values that were deemed to be important in society.

The law collections in our Bible, therefore, were never intended to be universally valid, but to address the problems facing the people of God at the time, as the differing laws regarding slave release show. Of course, some, like the Decalogue (the Ten Commandments), contain instructions that remain timeless because they deal with things that are wrong in any society, for example, murder and adultery. Others, like the commandment regarding Sabbath rest, provide us with valuable principles, such as treating one's dependents well. Others, however, such as those dealing with prisoners of war and chattel slavery, reflect the imperfect understanding and struggles of people learning to live as the people of God in their culture, and are not appropriate for our time.

In fact, the Old Testament also contains evidence that these voices of love and redemption were not always heard or appreciated by the Israelites themselves. Not only did chattel slavery exist, there is evidence that Israel did enslave its own people from time to time, despite the distaste for the practice expressed in the laws. For example, Nehemiah effectively

---

3. Bauckham, *The Bible in Politics*, 26.

conscripted people into his building project (Neh 4:16–22; 5:1–5). Solomon did the same; he had many men working on his mines and foundries (1 Kgs 5:13–15). Israel, like all other societies, had a long way to go before it was able to realize the values that were so important for it, and to understand how these values played out in practice. The law collections therefore record various voices and it is the modern reader's responsibility to try to discern which ones we should follow. We can learn much from the collections, and sometimes extract principles from them, but we should not view them as a block of legislation for absolute obedience in every age, for *they were never intended* to be seen as such in the first place.

Conclusion

What can the Old Testament say to us about slavery today? Although the worldview in which slavery is acceptable is attested and represented within our canon of Scripture, the voices that speak of freedom and justice, through which God's concern for the oppressed is heard, and that work against the forces that want to keep them that way, represent the truth of God's love for his people. It is to *these* voices that we must listen. Often, however, they can seem quieter and more subtle than those that bear witness to our human tendency to exploit and harm others for our own benefit. Perhaps this is partly because, like all human beings in every age, the Israelites took a long time to be able to discern these voices themselves. Throughout the Old Testament we see them struggling to understand what it means to be the people of God, and how to live lives according to his values while coping with the situation in which they find themselves. Perhaps it is partly because, as readers, we often are better able to hear the voices of human frailty than those that speak of love and justice, simply because we ourselves are human.

Today, it is our task as readers of Scripture to learn to listen to the redemptive voices and respond to them. It is tempting to be complacent and comfortable, and accept the values of our culture without questioning them. However, following the example of the prophets, we can speak out against the corruption, greed, and injustice that helps perpetuate slavery all over the world today. We can press for the changes in laws, which are necessary, while recognizing that any reforms that are made will be in themselves imperfect and inadequate. For, like the Hebrew legislators, we have an as yet imperfect understanding of how to respond to God's love for us.

We can identify with those that are considered dishonorable in society, seeing all people as children of God, and resisting the temptation to live lives in which wealth, honor, and status are prized. We can speak out for those who are oppressed, and work for the freedom of those who are in captivity. We can show that God is a God of redemption and justice, for whom exploitation of the poor and powerless is intolerable. And we can preach the good news of the one who comes to set the captives free.

 Questions for discussion.

1.   The story of the exodus was highly significant for the Hebrews. What significance might it have for our lives today?

2.   I have been suggesting that various voices can be heard throughout the Old Testament. To what extent do you find this idea helpful as you read Scripture?

3.   There are many laws in the Old Testament. How do you think Christians should view them today? Are they all to be adopted in our lives? If not, why not?

4.   The stories in the Old Testament tell us of values that were important to their narrators. What values do you detect in the Joseph story (Gen 37–50), for example?

5.   How can Christians follow the prophetic challenge to work against poverty and injustice?

6.   Why is the idea of a suffering servant so important for the Christian faith? Why do you think Isaiah speaks of a "suffering slave" and not a great king?

7.   Read the story of Naaman's slave-girl (2 Kgs 5:1–14). Can you discern the voice of love and justice in this story? How is it expressed?

5

SLAVERY IN THE
NEW TESTAMENT

Introduction

THE WORLD IN WHICH the New Testament writers lived was, in effect, made up of three groups of people—those who were free, those who were slaves, and former slaves who had been granted their freedom. Although slaves were at the bottom of the social pecking order, some could become influential in their own spheres, and even have slaves of their own. They could become physicians, civil servants, or secretaries, and those who developed such skills could be very valuable to their masters. Nevertheless, in a culture in which social honor was all-important, to be a slave was to be in a shameful position. Slaves and their families were the property of their masters. They had no identity of their own, were considered to be inherently inferior, and had no rights in society. Even those who gained their freedom through manumission (the technical term for granting a slave his or her freedom) always retained the shame of having been a slave. The whole of society's economic and political structures were built on the implicit belief not only that slaves were necessary, but that it was perfectly natural that some people should be enslaved.

Of course, the worldview of the first-century Graeco-Roman world regarding slavery is entirely foreign to most of us in the Western world today. Though some were disturbed by the cruel treatment of slaves and tried to deal with them humanely, it would never have occurred to them that this world order could be changed. In this chapter, we shall consider how the earliest Christians understood their lives within such a world. What difference did believing in Jesus make with regard to slavery in the first century, and what can we learn from this for today?

Jesus and Slavery

Since slavery played such an essential role in the first-century world, it is hardly surprising that slaves are frequently mentioned in the New Testament. In Matthew 26, the high priest's slave has his ear cut off, and later in the chapter, a slave-girl identifies Peter as having been with Jesus, which, of course, Peter then denies. In Acts 12:13–15 it is another slave-girl, named Rhoda, who recognizes Peter after he has escaped from prison. There are frequent references to slaves throughout the epistles and we know that there were both slaves and masters in the earliest congregations.

Slaves also appear in the stories Jesus tells. For example, in the Parable of the Weeds and the Wheat (Matt 13:24–30), it is slaves who spot that weeds have been planted in their owner's field. They wonder if they should pull up the weeds, but the master tells them not to, explaining that they might pull up the wheat along with them. In the Parable of the Talents, slaves are given the responsibility of looking after very large sums of money for their master (Matt 25:14–30). The severe punishment meted out to the one who merely hides the money, while the others invest it and make a profit for their master, would come as no surprise in a world in which harsh treatment of slaves was an everyday occurrence.

However, besides referring to slaves to illustrate his point, Jesus also frequently uses the idea of slavery as a metaphor to help people understand what it means to be his disciple. His followers are to think of themselves as his slaves, and so their lives must be characterized by service. They should be faithful, obedient, and loyal, serving Jesus by serving one another. They are to do this by being compassionate and merciful (Matt 18:23–25) and caring for their fellow believers (Matt 24:45–51; Luke 12:42–46). Like servants who have been put in charge of a house during their master's absence, they should be alert (Mark 13:33–37), attending to their work in the kingdom and watching for when their master returns home.

No one should think of himself or herself as higher than any other person, for Jesus' followers are all slaves, all equal. Indeed it goes further than this—there is actually a reversal of values. In the world, those considered to have honor are those who have wealth, superior status, and social influence. Under God's rule, however, things are the other way round. This is illustrated in the incident in which James and John, the sons of Zebedee, ask to sit on either side of Jesus when he is in glory (Mark 10:37). Jesus says he is not able to grant this and goes on to explain the way it should be among his followers. Rather than seeking honor, he says,

> Whoever wishes to become great among you must be your servant, and whoever wishes to be first among you must be slave of all. (Mark 10:43–44)

The disciples' lives must be characterized by humble service. Greatness does not mean lording it over others, reveling in status and honor. Why? Because Jesus himself came into the world to serve humanity, even to the extent of giving up his life.

> For the Son of Man came not to be served, but to serve, and to give his life a ransom for many. (Mark 10:45)

Followers of Jesus therefore need to learn completely new values, an entirely different way of thinking. They have to think of themselves as slaves (unthinkable in such a society), and Jesus is the example they are to follow.

Jesus the Redeemer

We saw in the last chapter that Isaiah spoke of the suffering slave who would come as the new Moses to rescue all his people from their own sin and from oppression. Throughout the New Testament it becomes clear that the early Christians believe that Jesus is that suffering slave (e.g., Matt 8:14–17; Luke 22:37; Acts 8:30–35; 1 Pet 2:21–25). The idea of Jesus as the redeemer is expressed in various ways. In Luke's Gospel, for example, Jesus declares that he is the fulfillment of the prophecy of Isaiah 61:2:

> The Spirit of the LORD is upon me,
> because he has anointed me to bring
> good news to the poor.
> He has sent me to proclaim release to the captives
> and recovery of sight for the blind,
> to let the oppressed go free,
> to proclaim the year of the Lord's favor. (Luke 4:18–19)

For Luke, Jesus is the one who will do all these things that Isaiah foretold. Matthew expresses the same idea, but rather differently. He tells the story of Jesus being taken to Egypt by Mary and Joseph in order to escape Herod, and explains that this fulfills the prophecy of Hosea 11:1—"out of Egypt have I called my son" (Matt 2:15). It seems that for Matthew, Jesus is to be the new Moses who leads his people from captivity to sin. According to Paul, Jesus will lead his people to freedom again (Rom 11:26 cf. Isa 59:20–21).

The idea that Jesus came into the world to be a servant to others, and that his disciples must do the same, is most clearly spelled out in Paul's letter to the Philippians. In chapter 2, Paul asks that the believers do not act out of selfish ambition or conceit, "but in humility regard others as better than yourselves" (Phil 2:3). He then goes on, in what is possibly an ancient hymn, to show that this is exactly what Jesus himself did, and that we should follow his example. He gave up his status in order to serve humanity, humbling himself in absolute obedience to God, even to the extent of dying a criminal's death on the cross. He was the King, but he became a slave, for the sake of God's people. This is the way that believers should live—serving one another, not grasping the social status they think they deserve, but giving it up for others.

Slavery in the Early Church

On several occasions, Paul, like Jesus, makes use of the idea of slavery as a metaphor for discipleship. He calls himself a "slave of Christ" (Rom 1:1; Gal 1:10; 2 Cor 6:2–4) in much the same way that the prophets understood themselves to be slaves of YHWH (Isa 49:3; Jer 7:25). But this is not a special status, for he says the same thing of all believers (1 Cor 7:22; Rom 14:18), who have been released from slavery to sin (Rom 8:2).

As we have seen with regard to Philippians 2, the equality of believers, and mutual service, are to be the hallmarks of the Christian community. Paul says something similar in Galatians 3:28. As he discusses questions about whether or not gentile believers should obey Jewish law, Paul declares that the categories of slave and free no longer exist. There is no reason why gentiles should have to adopt Jewish practices, because in Christ Jesus the old divisions are made obsolete.

> There is no longer Jew or Greek, there is no longer slave or free, there is no longer male and female; for all of you are one in Christ Jesus. (Gal 3:28)

Because of what Jesus has done, the things that divide people in society—race, social status, and gender—should no longer do so, for all are one in Christ Jesus. The question is, how did this extraordinary teaching actually play out in the church, in which real masters and slaves came together to worship? Did it mean that all Christian slaveholders should grant their slaves freedom? Should Christian slaves actively seek their freedom? How were masters and slaves to understand their relationship in the light of their belief in Christ?

These questions were bound to come up in his churches, and when they did, Paul's advice was sought. In the church at Corinth, questions arose with regard to both marriage and slavery. Some seem to have been wondering if married Christians should be celibate. Should marriage actually be discouraged? What about Christians married to unbelievers, should they get divorced? Should Jewish men try to remove the sign of their Judaism, circumcision? Should slaves try to gain their freedom? As a general rule, he says, do not to try to change your circumstances. Those who are unmarried should remain single (although he allows for the fact that some will want to marry), and those who are married to nonbelievers should not seek divorce. Jews should not become gentiles. Then in 1 Corinthians 7:21, he talks about slaves. "Were you a slave when you were called? Don't let it trouble you," he says, which seems to suggest that slaves should not seek their freedom. He goes on to explain what he means in the next verse. However, unfortunately, the Greek is unclear and can be translated in two different ways, as we can see by comparing the RSV and the NRSV. In the RSV we read, "But if you can gain your freedom, avail yourself of the opportunity." The NRSV, on the other hand, has "make use of your present condition now more than ever," which seems to suggest the opposite—that slaves should not look for freedom, but make the most of their situation for the sake of the gospel. If, as most commentators on the passage think, the RSV translation is the better one, then it seems that Paul is telling the Corinthian slaves that if the opportunity arises, they should take their freedom. Nevertheless, in verse 22, he reminds them that while freedom is desirable, they should not pursue it as their sole aim in life, for that would detract their attention from their real purpose, which is to serve Christ. All believers, whether owners or slaves, should think of themselves in this way: social status is ultimately a matter of indifference in the light of one's new identity in Christ. For, above and beyond the social status quo, there is an entirely different reality in which all are slaves of Jesus Christ. In the spiritual realm, there is no difference between slaves and free (7:22–23).

On another occasion, Paul had to deal with the problem of a runaway slave called Onesimus. The slave's master is one of Paul's converts, Philemon, and Paul's letter to him is preserved for us. In it, Paul seems to be urging Philemon to take his slave back, and asking him not to punish him because he should consider Onesimus a brother in Christ. If this is the right reading, it would be considered very radical in Paul's time, for runaway slaves could be punished very severely and even put to death. Such a gracious response would make sense in the light of Christ's mercy in the face of terrible sin. However, it may also be that when Paul urges Philemon to treat Onesimus "as a brother," he is actually asking him—albeit in an indirect manner—to free his slave. Either way, Paul is certainly asking Philemon to do something that would be out of the ordinary for his time.

Paul's responses to these real life situations suggest that when he says in Galatians 3:28 that "there is neither slave nor free," he is stating a spiritual truth: believers are of equal status because they are all slaves of Christ. However, he does not seem to be thinking that there should be an actual eradication of the difference between slaves and masters, any more than there should be between men and women. It seems quite likely that he would have preferred slaves to be set free, but he does not say this directly. What he does say is that believers should have a new understanding of themselves, which profoundly affects the way they understand and relate to each other. It is this that will produce a very different society from that to be found outside the church. The values of the world are turned upside down in the kingdom of God. High status, which is so important in the world, is considered to be shameful in the church, and low status, which is normally considered to be dishonorable, is respected. Thus, while Paul does not call for the eradication of slavery, he does, subtly, question the values that perpetuate it.

But how far did all this affect the real life of slaves in the churches? As the years progressed, it seems that Christians continued to struggle with living out their new beliefs. Although Paul may have thought it better for slaves to be freed, this may not have been a practical option for many. How would they earn a living once they were freed? How would they be able to pay the fee that slaves had to pay to their former owners? In everyday church life, therefore, the problem may not have been whether someone should be freed or not, but how masters and slaves who were now followers of Jesus should relate to each other. What difference should this make in their lives? So it is that we find there are instructions dealing with exactly that. For example, in Colossians, we read:

> Slaves, obey your earthly masters in everything, not only while being watched and in order to please them, but wholeheartedly fearing the Lord. Whatever your task, put yourselves into it, as done for the Lord and not for your masters, since you know that from the Lord you will receive the inheritance as your reward; you serve the Lord Jesus Christ. For the wrongdoer will be paid back for whatever wrong has been done, and there is no partiality. Masters, treat your slaves justly and fairly, for you know that you also have a Master in heaven. (Col 3:22—4:1)

At first sight this looks like the gospel, with its emphasis on reversal of status, has made no difference to the way they live, for slaves are to obey their masters. But these practical instructions for Christian households do reveal changes in the way followers of Jesus should think about their relationships with each other. First, lists like these (known as "household codes") were common in the ancient world, and it was highly unusual for slaves to be addressed in them at all. Second, the reason given for slaves to be obedient to their masters is striking. Instead of advising that they be obedient to gain favor from their masters, this writer tells them that they are to work to gain favor from Jesus himself. Thirdly, masters are reminded that they are to treat their slaves well, not because they think this is the way to have well-run households, but because this is part of their own service to Jesus Christ. Indeed, the letter to the Ephesians goes even further: *all* Christians are reminded that they should be subject to one another (5:21), treating each other with respect. For, the simple fact is, they all have the same master.

In 1 Timothy 6:1–2, however, things are a bit different. Here, slaves who have Christian masters are warned that they should not take advantage of their spiritual equality and show disrespect for their owners.

> All who are under the yoke of slavery should consider their masters worthy of full respect, so that God's name and our teaching may not be slandered. Those who have believing masters should not show them disrespect just because they are fellow believers. Instead, they should serve them even better because their masters are dear to them as fellow believers and are devoted to the welfare of their slaves.

The fact that there is no balancing instruction to masters to treat their slaves fairly has caused many to think that this is a step back from the teaching we find in Colossians and Ephesians. However, if as scholars think, the church was experiencing persecution at this time, it may have seemed sensible for them to "keep their heads down" and not to draw attention to themselves. It may have been that some slaves were aware of the teaching about spiritual equality and wanted to see it put into practice. Perhaps some of them were even taking advantage of this teaching, and showing disrespect to their masters. If this were the case, it certainly would not look good to people outside the church, especially at a time when Christians were increasingly seen as suspect. What kind of a group of people allows its slaves to be disrespectful? A bad reputation could undermine the effectiveness of the gospel message.

But what about the relationship between slaves who are Christians and their non-Christian masters? What happens if a non-Christian master ill-treats a Christian slave? How should the slave react? In 1 Peter, slaves are told that they are to be respectful even to those who ill-treat them. They are to remember that Christ was ill-treated, he endured injustice and did not seek any compensation for this. He simply endured and triumphed in the end, and this is what the slaves are to do too.

The New Testament Message about Slavery

In the last chapter we saw that the Old Testament writers lived in a world in which slavery was unquestioned. At no time did any of the Old Testament writers think that slavery was a bad idea, although there were challenges to this assumption, however imperfect we may think them today. The story of their own redemption from slavery underpinned the sense of justice that insisted that the poor should not be exploited, and the attempts to curtail the excesses of those who were in power. In Isaiah we saw that there was a belief that a new redeemer would come who would release the captives. He would be a suffering servant who would lead his people into freedom. In the New Testament we meet that suffering servant. Jesus, the redeemer, is the slave-king who comes to set the captives free. His followers have been given freedom to serve him and one another. We are all equal in his sight, all slaves of the one master.

However, despite this teaching, and the core values of freedom and equality that are part and parcel of it, it is never suggested in the New Testament that slavery should be ended. Jesus does not demand it. Paul may have suspected that this was the natural outcome of belief in Jesus (although we cannot be sure), however he seems to have been reluctant to say so outright. Despite the central teaching of Jesus as the redeemer, it seems never to have occurred to any of the earliest Christians that ending slavery might be a natural consequence of the teaching of the gospel. It is true that a couple of passages do speak of slave traders with disapproval. In 1 Timothy 1:9–10, slave traders are denounced as "lawless and disobedient": human trafficking is an extreme example of stealing. In Revelation 18:13, trading in human beings is the height of greed and is characteristic of the Empire in which Christians should have no part. However, this was a common belief about slave traders in the ancient world, who were generally distrusted, and need not necessarily be considered as a direct consequence of the gospel. The churches themselves do not seem to have thought it necessary or desirable to abolish slavery. The question is, why?

It is important to realize that to look for abolitionism within the New Testament is to try to read our own twenty-first-century values into the first century. We are so accustomed to a society without slavery that we naturally think that this is the way it should always be, and always should have been. However, in the first-century Graeco-Roman world, it would have been impossible to look for abolition as we know it today. It was quite simply unthinkable. For, as Richard Horsley says, "The only way of imagining a society without slavery would have been to imagine a different society."[1]

For anyone, even Jesus himself, to preach the abolition of slavery would have been to try to overturn social convention and practice in a way that would have been considered scandalous. They would have been laughed at, considered crazy, or even more dangerous than some people already thought them to be. In addition, promoting the abolition of slavery would have deflected attention from his main task of bringing the message of God's love to all people. And if the church had tried to do so, this would have taken away from their work of spreading the word about Jesus and nurturing those who became his disciples.

Nevertheless, awareness of just how entrenched slavery was in first century life helps us to see how extraordinary Jesus' teaching actually was. He constantly attacked religious power, which was so self-seeking. He identified with the poor and outcasts. He insisted on God's love for those at the bottom of the social scale. All this points to an extraordinary subversive voice of the sort we have become familiar with in the Old Testament. His depiction of his disciples as slaves, and his insistence that they too should not be taken in by the power structures of the world—that they too should not seek the kind of honor and glory that the world expects—was, as we know, deeply threatening to those who were in power, and it ultimately cost him his life. His challenging of those in his own religion who had turned it from a relationship with the redeeming God to a power-broking, self-serving, and oppressive force, was more than many could bear—and so he had to go.

Paul's understanding of the implications of Jesus' life and message are equally extraordinary. He understood that the saving work of the slave-king should have the effect of overturning the accepted norms of society, and that Jesus' power had been effective only through his weakness. But he too worked within the constraints of his culture, and only indirectly hinted at one natural implication of the gospel—that those currently in slavery might in fact be the ones with most honor in God's kingdom, and that Christians should think about the place of slavery in the church.

This brief survey of the New Testament reveals something very similar to what we saw in the Old. We have the voices that simply relate the reality of slavery in the first-century world. Then we have Jesus' voice, which challenges that reality, but it does so indirectly. He does not call for abolition,

1. Horsley, "The Slave Systems of Classical Antiquity," 59.

but declares that he comes as a redeemer and as a slave to serve others, and says that his disciples must follow his example, identifying with the poor and oppressed, rather than following the world's values of honor and status. Other voices attest to this message, voices that understand Jesus to be the One foretold by Isaiah, or the new Moses, or the servant king who gave up his divine status in order to bring God's salvation to the world.

We also, however (and this is crucial for our understanding of the Bible for contemporary human trafficking), have the voices of those who were struggling to understand the implications of their faith for life in the culture of their time. These voices show the weakness of human comprehension, and the struggle to survive in a world that does not hold the values they are trying to understand. The importance of this cannot be underestimated. Inevitably some compromises had to be made. This helps us to understand the instructions in the household codes that slaves should be obedient to their masters, instructions that were so disturbing to those caught up in slavery in the eighteenth and nineteenth centuries. They must be seen as appropriate to their time, the imperfect attempts of church leaders to help their congregations live out the gospel in their own time and culture. Like the Old Testament laws, they are not to be applied in a literal universalized way, but must be understood in the light of the central message of the love of God for his people.

Conclusion

There may be no command to abolish slavery in the New Testament, but there is a voice which proclaims freedom—and it does so loudly and clearly. As followers of Jesus, there is a moral imperative for us to listen to this voice and obey its call to set the captives free. However, the voice of freedom and love in the New Testament demands much more of us than simply proclaiming justice and working towards abolition. Our study of the New Testament suggests that Jesus calls those of us who wish to be his disciples to a much deeper commitment even than this. He demands changes in our attitudes, and indeed in the way that we live. If we consider ourselves to be disciples of Christ, then we should view ourselves as his slaves. And if we are his slaves then we should be following his example and living lives that do not seek the honor and status that are the values of the world.

The New Testament voice of love and redemption insists that followers of Jesus serve others as he does, identifying with those who are oppressed and held captive. The temptation is always to be among the rich and powerful, but the New Testament teaches that those whom the world thinks powerful and honorable are actually the weakest in God's sight. On the other hand, those whom the world thinks to be weakest turn out to be the ones through whom God works. The truly great are those at the bottom of the social heap, for it is those whom Jesus identified with and came to save. This is a hard lesson to grasp and live out. It can be costly and even dangerous, for it is not a popular one in the world or even the church. By setting ourselves up as disciples of Jesus we are speaking out directly against the values of the world, and as the first Christians found, we often compromise in order to survive. However, it is by "having the same mind" as Christ (Phil 2:5) that God's message of redemption will be heard in the world. Thus, the question for the modern church is—are we prepared to listen to the voice of love and redemption (which is the voice of Jesus Christ himself), and to identify with the poor and oppressed, and to set the captives free? Are we prepared to let go of our own need for security and honor and be those who live out the values that are central to the gospel?

 Questions for discussion.

1. Read Philippians 2:5–11. What are the implications of the paradox of Christ as a slave-king for our church life today?

2. Think about people you know, or have read about, who embody gospel values in their lives. What do you admire in them, and why?

3. What does the idea of being a "slave of Christ" mean to you?

4. How should we understand the ideas of freedom and equality in our Christian lives?

5. Why, according to the New Testament, is slavery incompatible with a Christian worldview?

6. Read Mark 10:41–45. How do you think Jesus' words should be understood in the church today?

7. Why do you think Jesus did not directly condemn slavery?

8.   Read Colossians 3:22–24. For many Christians today, this passage can be applied to their employment situations. They understand it to mean that they should obey their employers and do their best at their work. Someone who is or has been a slave, however, might understand this passage differently. What would you say to them?

6

PROSTITUTION IN THE OLD TESTAMENT

Introduction

IN HIS BOOK *THE Natashas*, Viktor Malarek tells the story of Marika. Marika is Ukrainian, and very poor. She was offered a job in Tel Aviv as a waitress, which she accepted because she was desperate for work. However, she ended up in a locked flat and was forced to work as a prostitute. Recalling her arrival in the brothel, Marika says,

> That night, I felt for the first time what it was to be a whore. I had to service eight men. I felt so terrible and ashamed. I showered after every encounter but I could not wash away the filth in me. Over the next few months, I don't know how many hundreds of Israeli men I was forced to have sex with. Young men, old men, fat disgusting men. Soldiers, husbands, and religious men. It did not matter if I was sick or was on my period. I had to work or I would be punished.[1]

Marika speaks of feeling disgust and shame because of what she is made to do. The feeling of disgust is understandable, but why should Marika feel shame? What has she done wrong? Her sense of shame reflects the fact that in most societies, prostitution is seen as shameful, and historically, the church has associated it with sin. However, Marika's story should raise

1. Malarek, *The Natashas*, xiii.

questions for the church. Are prostitutes sinners? What should our view of prostitution be?

If we are at all concerned about sex trafficking, it is important that we address such questions, for two reasons. First, we may have unconscious attitudes to prostitution that hinder a compassionate response to victims of sex trafficking. Second, we need to be well informed. Many people argue that if prostitution were legalized, there would be no need for illegal brothels like the one Marika was kept in, and so sex trafficking would be reduced. Others think it would be much more effective to prosecute those who buy sex. How should Christians respond? In this chapter and the next, we will ask what the Bible might have to say about these questions. As before, we will start with the Old Testament, conducting a brief survey of passages in which prostitution is mentioned.

First, however, we need to be clear what we are talking about, for there is a problem with terminology. In English versions of the Old Testament, two Hebrew words have been translated as "prostitute"—*qĕdēšâ* and *zônā*. The term *zônā* refers to the prostitute as we would understand this today, while *qĕdēšâ* which means "consecrated one" or "holy one," has often been translated as "male cultic prostitute." In the NIV translation of 1 Kings 14:23–24, for example, we read that there were male shrine prostitutes in Judah during the reign of Rehaboam, and in 15:11–12 we are told that Asa expelled them. This translation of *qĕdēšâ* reflects a longstanding belief amongst Old Testament scholars that cultic prostitution was a feature of ancient Near Eastern religions, and that sometimes these practices found their way into Israelite religion too. Recently, however, this view has been challenged, for no evidence has been found to support the idea that cultic prostitution was ever a feature of these ancient religions. In fact, no one really knows who the people referred to as *qĕdēšîm* (the plural form of the Hebrew word) were or what their function was. We do know that the Old Testament writers always regard them with disapproval, but we cannot say any more than this. Accordingly, in line with this current scholarly thinking, in this chapter we will consider only those passages in which the term *zônā* appears in the Hebrew text.

Prostitution in the Laws

In Leviticus, three laws deal with prostitution directly. First, in Leviticus 19:29 it is forbidden for men to make their daughters work as prostitutes.

Two reasons are given. The girl would be "profaned" (NRSV). In other words, working as a prostitute would mean that she could not be considered pure or holy. Moreover, the whole country would be affected, for this would not only be a matter of individual holiness. Any father who did this would be introducing something (prostitution) into the country that would undermine the wellbeing of everyone in the land and affect their relationship with God.

Secondly, in Leviticus 21:7, 14 we read that priests should not marry prostitutes (or women who have been divorced). Priests must be meticulous about sexual purity, for they must not bring any impurity into the sanctuary. To ensure this, they must marry only virgins. Thirdly, in Leviticus 21:9 we read that if a priest's daughter becomes a prostitute she must be put to death. What the priest's family does will not only bring honor or dishonor to him, it will affect his purity and his ability to work in the sanctuary. But why should this be so? Leviticus 10:14 tells us that when the priest's family eats the food that is offered to God, they are to eat it in a ceremonially clean place. Contamination can creep into the sanctuary via the priest's family, so they must be pure too. The same association may be behind the rather strange instruction in Deuteronomy 23:18 that any earnings made from prostitution must not be brought to the sanctuary—this "dirty money" has no place there.

It is clear from these laws that prostitution was considered to be an undesirable element in society, and that the lawmakers thought it should be controlled. In large part, the associations of prostitution with impurity, dishonor, and shame, would be very effective in doing this. Prostitutes, who were considered to be the source of the danger, were shunned, kept as far away as possible from all that was considered good and pure. However, there were other ways of keeping prostitution under control. For example, there should, in theory, have been no need for men to visit prostitutes: men could sleep with their female slaves and could take other women as extra wives (concubines). Men were also responsible for ensuring that the women of their households were properly cared for, and, in the normal run of things, there should have been no need for women to resort to prostitution. Nevertheless, some could find themselves in circumstances in which they were no longer under that protection, for example, through widowhood or divorce, and in such situations prostitution might have been the only way they could survive.

Prostitution in the Narratives

That some did have to work in prostitution is attested to by several stories. In Judges 11:1, Jephthah's mother is said to be a prostitute. We learn in Judges 16:1 that Samson visited a prostitute: this great leader of Israel tended to be weak when faced with sexual temptation, and this would later bring about his downfall. In 1 Kings 3:16–28, two women who are described as prostitutes come to Solomon to help them settle a dispute. One woman accuses the other, whose own infant has died, of stealing her baby. Solomon solves the problem, and demonstrates his great wisdom by suggesting that the surviving child be cut into two pieces, which, of course, is unacceptable to the real mother. Prostitute she may be, but she loves her child. In fact, however, the two women's occupation adds very little to the story, except perhaps to illustrate that the lowest in society were able to approach the king for justice. There are two stories, however, in which women who are engaged in or are associated with prostitution are the main characters, and their association with or engagement in prostitution is highly significant. The first is found in Genesis 38 and tells of Tamar, the widow of Judah's son. The second is the story of Rahab, which is found in Joshua chapter 2.

The Story of Tamar

Tamar is the daughter-in law of the patriarch Judah. However, her husband dies, leaving her a childless widow. According to the tradition known as Levirate marriage (Deut 25:5–10), Tamar should sleep with her dead husband's brother in order to ensure that the family line would be continued. However, Judah's older son refuses to sleep with Tamar, and subsequently dies. The patriarch, worried that his third son (who is called Shelah) might die too, does not demand that he carry out this duty. So Tamar takes matters into her own hands. When Judah goes to Timnah where the sheep shearing is taking place, she sits at the side of the road and pretends to be a prostitute, hiding her face with a veil. Sure enough, when Judah sees her, he propositions her. Saying that he cannot pay her there and then, he gives her his seal, cord, and staff as a guarantee of payment the next day. So, Tamar sleeps with Judah. However, the following day, when Judah's friend goes to give the woman a goat in payment for her services, she is nowhere to be found. Judah decides not to pursue the matter, perhaps because he does not want people to know that this woman is in possession of his personal identification. As a result of the encounter, Tamar becomes pregnant. But when this is discovered, she is denounced as having "played the whore" by the other women of the household. (We do not know whether they are aware of what she has done, or are simply accusing her of illicit sexual activity.) Judah pronounces that she must be put to death. Tamar, however, sends him the cord, seal, and staff and says that the person who is the father of the child is the owner of these items. Judah realizes that he has been duped and says that she is more righteous than he is because she has ensured the continuation of the family line, something he himself had not made any effort to do. Tamar becomes the mother of twins, and one, Perez, becomes the ancestor of King David.

This story tells us a great deal about attitudes towards prostitutes in ancient Israel. As in many places in the world today, prostitutes worked at the side of the road where men would proposition them. Festivals and business occasions were prime occasions for prostitutes to make money. However, they did so outside the walls of cities or towns, for they were not considered part of decent society. As today, there were double standards. Women who were considered to have committed sexual sins were branded as prostitutes, as whores. Tamar's pregnancy is considered to be so shameful that she must be executed. However Judah, who has purchased sex from a supposed prostitute, goes without blame. His behavior seems to be considered normal.

But besides showing us a glimpse of the sexual mores of this time in history, the story also invites us to question them. Women were considered to be inferior to men, under their protection, and were expected to be obedient and loyal to them. As we have seen, maintaining the honor of the household was a male responsibility, while women looked after the domestic arrangements. In such a world, it was natural that Tamar should be punished, for she was thought to bring shame on the household. In this story, however, a different tale is told. Here, the male is in the wrong, for he fails to ensure that his family line is continued. Tamar is shown to be much cleverer and more moral than her father-in-law, for Judah's family line is only continued because of what she does. Judah, by contrast, comes across as rather stupid, lazy, fearful, and easily duped (he clearly didn't know Tamar very well or surely he would have recognized her). In the end he has to declare that this woman is more righteous than he is. So, the woman who is thought to be the lowest of the low is actually the one who rescues the great patriarch, Judah, from himself, and plays a crucial role in the history of Israel.

The Story of Rahab

In Joshua chapter 2, we read the story of the Canaanite prostitute Rahab. One day two Israelite men are sent by Joshua into Canaan. Their task is to spy out the land, in preparation for invasion. However, the first thing they do is go to Rahab's house—in other words, they go to a brothel. The king of Canaan learns that they are there and demands that Rahab hand them over to him. Instead, however, Rahab hides them in the roof-space of her house. She tells them that the Canaanites have heard of the way that YHWH, Israel's God, rescued them from Egypt. The Canaanites are afraid of Israel, because they know that God guides them. She asks that her family be spared when the invasion takes place. The two men assure her of this, and ask in return that she keep quiet about their whereabouts. Rahab helps them escape and the Israelites go on to defeat and occupy Canaan. Rahab and her family are kept safe and they are allowed to live in Israel (Josh 6:15–25).

Like the story of Tamar, this tale also helps us to understand attitudes to prostitution in Old Testament times, and it, too, questions them in an ingenious way. As a prostitute, Rahab must live and work on the outskirts of the town, for her occupation is shameful. Even though she plays a major role in Israel's history, her shame will never leave her: she is always known as "Rahab the prostitute." However, the fact that men should use her services is apparently unremarkable. On the surface of things, these double standards are not questioned, but when we dig a bit deeper, we find that the narrator is making some rather subtle points. The story contains many ironies, in much the same way as that of Tamar. Rahab is much cleverer than the spies. The men are supposed to be working, but the first thing they do when they go into Canaan is go to a brothel! Rahab is able to support her family because of men like these, whose behavior means that they are found out as soon as they enter Canaan. Like Tamar, she knows how exploitable male lust is. She also knows and understands about the God of Israel, even though she is a gentile. She helps the spies escape, protects her family, and ensures victory for Israel, all at the same time. She not only gets what she wants, she even becomes an ancestor of David. On the other hand, the spies, who should have been commended for their bravery and skill, end up having to be rescued by a prostitute!

Both stories challenge the accepted order. Men are not necessarily superior to women, and women can be shrewd, clever, and get the better of them. The stories make fun of male sexual weakness, and expose double standards. They demonstrate that those who are considered shameful in society can be used by God and be much cleverer than those whom society thinks are honorable. The accepted values of society may not always hold true. The person who is assumed to behave badly is the very one whom God honors. Things may not be as they seem.

"Playing the Harlot"

Throughout the Old Testament the idea of prostitution is used as a metaphor. In older translations the phrase used is "playing the harlot" or "playing the whore." In newer translations, such as the NRSV, we find the phrase "prostituting themselves." Sometimes, the idea means simply that someone is accused of sexual impropriety or promiscuity, as may be the case in the Tamar story. In Deuteronomy 22:19–21, for example, if a woman is found not to be a virgin when she gets married, she is said to have "played the harlot." Mainly, however, the phrase is used metaphorically to refer to idolatry, either in the form of worshipping pagan gods, or simply when people follow their own desires, rather than serve God. For example, in Exodus 34:15–16, Israel is said to play the harlot or prostitute herself by worshipping pagan gods. In Leviticus 20:6 consulting mediums is said to be "playing the harlot."

The idea of prostitution as a metaphor for idolatry and disobedience to God is found especially in the prophets. In Isaiah 1:21 (cf. 57:3), for example, Jerusalem is said to be a harlot because the people are dabbling in pagan ritual. As a result, there is injustice in the city. In Isaiah 23:15–17 the same thing is said of the city of Tyre, but this time it is greed that is described as harlotry—the city's commercial success means that its citizens have gone after the things that they want, rather than obey God. In Nahum 3, Nineveh is said to be like a prostitute who will be punished for her behavior.

The most well-known use of the metaphor of prostitution is in the prophecy of Hosea. There it is used in conjunction with the idea that YHWH has entered into a marriage covenant with his people. Hosea is instructed by God to marry Gomer who is described as a "woman of promiscuity." The phrase does not necessarily mean that she is a prostitute, but that she stands for all that is idolatrous. Gomer represents Israel, which has become ensnared in pagan worship, and there is a "spirit of fornication" in the land. In other words, her activities have contaminated the whole people. She is like a prostitute who is looking for customers and she is bringing harm upon herself in the process, as well as breaking her marriage covenant with

YHWH. Gomer (Israel) is threatened with terrible punishment in an effort to make her change her behavior (2:3) and turn back to Him.

A similar idea is found in Jeremiah 2:20 in which Israel is said to have played the whore under "every green tree," that is, she is worshipping the pagan god Ba'al. As a result, innocent people are being hurt (2:34): the lack of faithfulness of the religious leaders and other powerful people is harming those who are most vulnerable in society. Behavior of this kind pollutes society, which must be cleansed of it. Here, YHWH is said to divorce Israel (3:8).

In Ezekiel, the metaphor of harlotry is taken to extremes. In chapter 16, Jerusalem, which is likened to an abandoned baby, is rescued and cared for by God. He enters into a covenant with her and she becomes a beautiful queen. However, she forgets God and all that he has done for her. She becomes a prostitute, making idols out of her jewelry, and even sacrificing her children. She is said to be highly promiscuous and her lovers are the neighboring countries. That is, she makes alliances with countries whose values are opposed to God's. A similar story is told of Samaria and Jerusalem in chapter 23, but here the two cities are said to be YHWH's daughters, Oholah and Oholibah, whose behavior is highly depraved. In both chapters, then, debased sexual behavior, including prostitution and promiscuity, is used as a metaphor to describe unfaithfulness to God. It is used in contrast with another metaphor, that of marriage, which is used for the intimate relationship that God wants with his people, a relationship that is broken by their unfaithfulness.

In Ezekiel, as in Hosea, this kind of behavior is said to deserve harsh punishment—so harsh that it is still deeply shocking to us today. In part, Oholah and Oholibah will bring that punishment on themselves, for their behavior will have serious consequences: the world of prostitution tends to be very violent. As in real life, customers and pimps can turn on the women—rape and murder are not uncommon. These metaphorical prostitutes will be horribly punished for their behavior: their nose and ears will be cut off, and they will be humiliated, raped, and robbed by their customers and lovers. Not only that, however, God himself threatens to punish them. Idolatry must be exposed, its perpetrators humiliated, and their reputation ruined. Then, perhaps, God's people will return to him.

The metaphor of the harlot has a dual purpose. It is used to speak of Israel's rebellion, but it is intended also to remind us of God's great love for his people. It is used as a warning to those in power to maintain the covenant with God and ensure their own welfare and that of their people. Rebellion against God will bring about disaster. It will bring injustice and great suffering for the poor. Such infidelity is in sharp contrast to YHWH's great love—he longs for his people to be in intimate relationship with him.

Wisdom Literature

The style of the book of Proverbs is quite different from the shocking, dramatic language that characterizes the prophets. Here, instead of vivid imagery and emotionally charged tirades, we have collections of sayings that have been built up over centuries. These sayings give common sense advice for living life well. The first nine chapters of the book form a distinct group, and address a young man. He is warned against wicked men who will lead him into paths of crime, laziness, and corruption. He is also warned against a "strange woman," who could lead him into committing adultery. This is a married woman, again a metaphor, who is in contrast to the pure woman, who is "lady wisdom." The "strange woman" is said to dress immodestly, like a prostitute, and he is warned against her, for she could lead him into committing adultery (7:10).

It might seem odd that adultery is considered more dangerous than visiting prostitutes (6:26). Why? Sleeping with a prostitute is a foolish short-term assignation. Adultery, however, ruins the very fabric of family life. An affair with a married woman is likely, according to this verse, to end up in a long-term obligation to keep her in the style to which she has become accustomed. However, this does not mean that visiting prostitutes is approved of. Prostitution is mentioned in this verse merely to make a point about the dangers of adultery. Elsewhere, there are warnings. In 23:27–28, a prostitute is described as a "deep pit." Men who become involved with prostitutes risk becoming ensnared in something from which they cannot escape. What seems attractive in the short term could lead to long-term disaster. The thrill and risk of impersonal sexual encounters could become addictive, not to mention the fact that spending too much money on prostitutes could lead to financial ruin and the loss of a good reputation (29:3).

Prostitution, Impurity, and Corruption

Although it is clear that, for the Old Testament writers, prostitution represents impurity and danger, it is not immediately obvious why. We can perhaps gain some understanding by looking at some laws that concern sexual behavior and reproduction. Firstly, sexual activity of any kind was associated with uncleanness. According to Leviticus 15:18, after sexual intercourse, a married couple is considered unclean until evening (as is any man who has an emission of semen). Secondly, anything to do with the female reproduction system is associated with impurity. When a woman has her period (Lev 15:19–24) or gives birth she is considered to be unclean. In fact, women were associated with impurity right from the time of their birth. We can begin to see why prostitutes were shunned and kept away from what was supposed to be pure—as a promiscuous woman who was likely to bear many children, the prostitute was unclean much of the time.

However, prostitution was not only considered to be a ritual sin, it was also a moral sin, which was believed to corrupt the whole land. As we have seen from the prophetic literature, prostitution was associated with lawlessness and violence. In addition, in a culture in which families and family lines were so important, women who lived and raised children outside the accepted structures of society may have been felt to have been a threat to a well-ordered society.

The Old Testament and Today's Sex Industry

Throughout the Old Testament there is a strong tradition that prostitution is an undesirable element in society. This was clearly the dominant cultural view and there seems to be no voice that challenges that common perception. There seems, therefore, to be no support within the Old Testament for the idea that such a thing as a "sex industry" should be accepted or that prostitution is a legitimate occupation for a woman to choose. There is, however, an acceptance that prostitution would always exist in society and that the best way to deal with it was to try and control it. Like most societies before and since, the Old Testament leaders seem to have taken the view that the best way to do this was to punish the prostitutes themselves. In the main, this took the form of stigmatizing the women involved, but there is also a lot of evidence that promiscuous women were believed to deserve very harsh physical punishment—even capital punishment.

Does this mean that the same approach should be taken today? Ought we to try to curtail the sex industry by punishing prostitutes? Some might think that this is suggested in the laws and the prophetic passages that we have been considering. We might be tempted to think that because God threatens the prostitutes with humiliation and harsh punishment, we should be doing the same thing today. There are, however, several reasons why this would not be an appropriate conclusion to draw.

First, the laws regarding prostitution, like those dealing with slavery, have to be seen against their cultural background, and we should not try to universalize them as commandments to be obeyed today. While we might agree that men should not put their daughters into prostitution, we would scarcely think it right to put the daughter of a minister or pastor to death for working in prostitution (or even, for that matter, for being promiscuous). Not only would we come up against legal objections, this would hardly be in line with the "law of love."

Second, the same thing applies to the passages in the prophets that use the harlotry metaphor. Of course, the prophets' message contains ideas that have universal relevance and remain central to the way Christians should live in the world; for example, their insistence that God's people should care for the poor and speak out against injustice. But to think that those passages in which God threatens prostitutes with violence mean that we should do likewise would be seriously to misunderstand their message. The prophets were warning against the unfaithfulness, disobedience, and sin that damage the relationship between God and his people. In order to get their message across they used ideas that they knew would get the attention of their listeners, which the harlotry metaphor certainly does.

This important point for us, however, is that the harlotry metaphor is just that—a metaphor. It is not to be taken literally. Unfortunately, it is easy for modern readers to forget this. This could be because we become so caught up in the violence and drama of the passage that we lose sight of the fact of its metaphorical nature. Or, alternatively, we could be so familiar with the texts that we take them literally, as if the events really happened. Either way, we are missing the point that the prophets are trying to make.

Third, the prophets use the harlotry metaphor because of its powerful resonances with impurity in Jewish tradition. It exploits deep-seated fears, and is designed to persuade those who hear the message to change their behavior. The threats of violence, which seem so excessive and distasteful to us today, have the same aim in view. However, the sheer violence of the threats is the giveaway that these passages are not to be taken literally—for if God did what he threatened, Israel would no longer exist and this would, of course, be in direct contradiction to the claim that he longs for his people to return to him!

All this points us to the fact that these passages are not about prostitution at all, but about a righteous God who cannot stand the behavior of those who say they are his followers but whose actions are contrary to all that he demands of them. The idea that these passages teach that God wants prostitutes to be punished severely misses the point entirely, and tells us more about the one drawing such a conclusion than it does about the Bible or the God whom we profess to worship.

Conclusion

As we saw with regard to slavery, different voices and traditions are represented within the biblical texts. On the one hand, some reflect the norms of society, with all its double standards and injustices. On the other hand, these norms are challenged, urging us to go deeper and discern the voices that reflect God's great love for his people. Certainly, with regard to prostitution, the cultural voices are very loud indeed, such as those that seem to suggest that prostitutes should be punished and considered scapegoats for society's ills. However, we should not allow them to drown out the quieter, challenging voices. These quieter voices are to be heard, I suggest, in the stories that expose double standards and make fun of the view that women in general (let alone prostitutes) are morally inferior to the men who have responsibility in society, and in the wisdom tradition which warns men to take responsibility for their own actions. These voices continually undermine popular ideas of what is shameful and what is not. The powerful and emotive language of louder cultural voices is often very attractive, but this, as we now know, might not be compatible with the law of love. Already in the Old Testament we can hear the voice of redemption for Marika and the many thousands who find themselves trapped in the sex industry.

 Questions for discussion.

1. Why did the Old Testament writers view prostitution as an undesirable element in society?

2. What are we to make of the prophets' harsh language about prostitutes and prostitution?

3. Throughout the Old Testament, double standards regarding how men and women are viewed are exposed and challenged. Where are there double standards in the church today and how can you go about tackling them?

4. What distinction does the Old Testament make between prostitution and prostitutes?

5. What are the "cultural voices" currently in your own society/church/community with regard to prostitution and those caught up in it?

6. Read the story of Tamar and Judah (Gen 38). What assumptions are challenged by its "subversive voice"?

7. Rahab and Tamar become ancestors of King David and of Jesus himself. How do you react to the idea that these women are honored by God?

8. Are there any individuals or groups in your community, family, or society, who are treated as scapegoats by others? If so, why, and what can you do about it?

7

PROSTITUTION IN THE NEW TESTAMENT

Introduction

IN *CASTING STONES*, RITA Nakashima Brock and Susan Brooks Thistlethwaite tell of an incident that took place while they were doing research for their book. During a visit to a church, one of the authors told the congregation about her work with women in prostitution. She was asked not take the women there as it would "spoil the image" of the church. This reaction is not at all uncommon. While there are many Christians who feel a compassionate concern for those caught up in prostitution, there are many more who see them as "fallen women," the worst of sinners. Women who work in prostitution, even those like Marika who are forced to do so against their will, are consequently shunned and even excluded from the church.

The figure of Mary Magdalene from the Gospels, who until recently was thought of as the patron saint of "repentant whores," has been used to support the view of prostitutes as fallen women, and historically, the church has hidden them away and tried to reform them in institutions such as the "Magdalene laundries." Today, prostitution tends to be something of a taboo subject within most church circles—too embarrassing or distasteful to talk about. In the secular world, it is common practice in many societies to prosecute people who work as prostitutes, and this can be a serious problem for those who wish to leave prostitution. Both the stigma and the criminal record can mean that they find it very difficult to find other employment.

It is crucial that we are aware of our own attitudes as we prepare to read the New Testament and to realize that we may have unconsciously absorbed certain preconceived ideas or prejudices about prostitution. It is helpful to examine ourselves—what are our attitudes towards those involved in prostitution? So we have to ask: do we really know what the Bible has to say on the subject, or do we merely *think* we know? As we turn to the New Testament we will again follow the example of the abolitionists, making a conscious effort to listen for the voice of love and redemption, in order to help us think about how we can respond to the injustice and suffering endured by the victims of sex trafficking today.

Prostitution in the Gospels

For much of Christian history, there has been a commonly held belief that Jesus, in his earthly ministry, was particularly close to women in prostitution and that he offered them a special grace. In large part, this stems from the tradition that two women in the Gospels, Mary Magdalene and the woman who anoints Jesus' feet and washes them with her hair, were prostitutes. However, as we shall see, there is little or no evidence for this in the Bible itself. As far as Mary Magdalene is concerned, the Gospels tell us that she, along with other women, looked after Jesus' needs during his ministry in Galilee (Matt 27:55–56; John 19:25). According to Luke 8:1–3, she had had seven demons cast out of her. In Mark 15:40–41 we learn that she was one of a group of women who watched the crucifixion from a distance.

In Mark and Luke, she and others go to anoint Jesus' body, only to be told by two men in bright shining clothes that Jesus was risen (Mark 16:1–2; Luke 24:1–10, but cf. Matt 28:1 which says only that they went to look at the tomb). According to John, however, she goes alone, and meets Jesus himself (John 20:1–18), thus becoming the first witness to the resurrection.

Mary Magdalene was obviously a very important figure in Jesus' life and ministry. She has been called the "apostle to the apostles" because she was the first to tell the disciples that Jesus had risen from the dead. Nowhere, however, is it said that she was a prostitute. In support of the idea, it has been suggested that the demons that were cast out must have included lust, but there is no evidence for this. Similarly, Jesus' words to Mary in John 20:17 ("do not touch me"), have been taken to refer to touch of a sexual nature. But the Greek is more likely to mean "do not hold on to me," suggesting that she must not try to prevent him from going back to the Father.

The story of the woman who anoints Jesus was clearly very significant for the earliest Christians, for it is told in each of the Gospels. The variations in the accounts probably reflect changes that took place as the story was told over the years (Luke 7:36–50; Mark 14:3–9; Matt 26:6–13; John 12:1–8). In John 12:1–8, Jesus is at Lazarus' house in Bethany, and the woman who anoints him is Mary, the sister of Martha. In the other Gospels, however, the woman is unnamed. In the Luke version, Jesus is a guest at a Pharisee's house. A woman who is known as a "sinner" brings an alabaster jar of ointment to the house, and bathes Jesus' feet with her tears, drying them with her hair, and anointing them with the ointment. The Pharisee doubts that Jesus can be a prophet, because if he were he would know what kind of woman this is, and would not have allowed her to touch him. Jesus tells the story of the two debtors, and points out that the one who has had the greater debt cancelled will love the creditor more. So it is with the woman. Simon has not given him water for his feet. He did not kiss him, or anoint him with oil. The woman, however, has done all these things. Her many sins have been forgiven, and so she has shown great love. In the Mark and Matthew versions (Mark 14:3–9; Matt 26:6–13), Simon is not a Pharisee but a leper. A woman pours ointment on Jesus' head and some who are present (the disciples in Mark) become angry at the waste, saying the ointment could have been sold and the money given to the poor. Jesus says they will always have the poor with them and that she has anointed his body prior to his burial.

Here again, it is nowhere said that this woman who anoints Jesus is a prostitute. However, the idea seems to have come about primarily because she is said to be a "sinner" in the Luke version of the story. But why should the word "sinner" mean that she is a prostitute? Some have suggested that only a prostitute would unbind her hair in public, while others have thought that her wiping of Jesus' feet is a particularly sensuous act. But neither need necessarily mean that she is a prostitute. We are left wondering—if this woman was a prostitute, why didn't the Gospel writers say so?

Despite the fact that neither Mary Magdalene nor the women who anoints Jesus is said to be a prostitute in the Gospels themselves, the idea has been very influential indeed. In part, it can be traced back to an early tendency to confuse the two women, seeing them as one and the same. This is seen in these words of Pope Gregory the Great (c. 540–604), who declared:

> She whom Luke calls the sinful woman, whom John calls Mary, we believe to be the Mary from whom seven devils were ejected according to Mark. And what did these seven devils signify, if not all the vices? . . . It is clear, brothers, that the woman previously used the unguent to perfume her flesh in forbidden acts.[1]

It is evident from this homily that Pope Gregory thinks that this woman was the archetypal sinner, and it is interesting to see how he highlights sexual sin here. To a large extent, this reflects the medieval idea that sexuality was the result of the Fall and the belief that chastity was necessary for holiness. Mary Magdalene, who became the model for "repentant whores" was seen as the opposite of the Virgin Mary. However, the notion has not

---

1. Homily XXXIII. Quoted in Haskins, *Mary Magdalene*, 93.

been confined to the Middle Ages, for it has been fascinating novelists, artists, and film makers even up to the present day (think, for example, of the musical "Jesus Christ Superstar"). The idea of Mary Magdalene as a "fallen woman" is a powerful one, but it probably owes more to the church's imagination than to any historical fact.

Prostitution in Jesus' Teaching

The idea that the "repentant whore" receives special forgiveness from Jesus may have been the stuff of legend for Christians throughout the centuries, but it has little or no grounding in the Gospels themselves. In fact, the word for prostitute (*pornē*) occurs only three times in the Gospels (Matt 21:31–32; Luke 15:30). In Matthew 21, Jesus has been telling the chief priests and elders the story of a man who has two sons. The father asks the first son to go and work in the vineyard. Initially he refuses, but later changes his mind and goes to work as he is told. Then the father asks the second son to work in the vineyard. This son says he will go, but does not. Jesus asks them which of the two sons did what the father wanted, and the answer, of course, is that the first son did so. Jesus then says,

> Truly I tell you, the tax collectors and the prostitutes are going into the kingdom of God ahead of you. For John came to you in the way of righteousness and you did not believe him, but the tax collectors and the prostitutes believed him; and even after you saw it, you did not change your minds and believe him. (Matt 21:31–32)

Jesus' point seems to be that those who appear to be sinners might just be the ones who will go into the kingdom of God, or, to put it another way, they may turn out to have a much greater understanding of what God's rule means than the religious authorities do. Anyone who thinks he is righteous should beware.

The word *pornē* appears also in the Parable of the Prodigal Son (Luke 15:30). A man has two sons, the younger of whom asks for his share of his inheritance, and squanders it all in wild living. When famine comes he gets a job looking after pigs. When he becomes so hungry that he wants to eat the animals' food, he realizes that he would be much better off at home, working as a hired hand. His father welcomes him back with open arms and throws a lavish party to celebrate. The older brother meanwhile, refuses to go to the party, protesting bitterly that no celebration has ever been given for him. He has been working for years, he says to his father, "but when this son of yours who has squandered your property with prostitutes comes home, you kill the fattened calf for him!" (Luke 15:30). This accusation is interesting. Jesus has not said that the younger son visited any prostitutes, but that he became caught up in "wild living." Prostitution may have been involved, but we cannot be sure. At any rate, the obedient older son cannot think of anything worse to say about his brother—he has squandered all his money on prostitutes!

In both of these passages, Jesus refers to prostitutes as an example of people classed as sinners and social outcasts. In Matthew 21 they are mentioned alongside tax collectors, who are generally despised because of their wheeling and dealing. In the Parable of the Prodigal Son they are classed as part of a world of degradation and sin. In each case, prostitutes represent those who are considered by religious people and society as a whole to be shameful, without honor. It would be a mistake, however, to infer from this that Jesus thinks that prostitutes should be stigmatized because of their shameful status in the world. For Jesus is calling the religious leaders' bluff—*they* are the ones who think prostitutes and tax collectors are excluded from the kingdom of God. They think that those who live religiously and morally impeccable lives are the ones whom God favors, while those whose sins may be more obvious are rejected. For Jesus, however, such assumptions are hypocritical and must be challenged.

Judging from these few verses, and from the Jewish tradition to which Jesus belonged, it seems that he would consider prostitution to be part of a world that is living outside of the will of God. He would therefore take the view that it was an undesirable element in society, for all the reasons we saw in the last chapter. However, he does not single it out as a particularly serious kind of sin as compared to others.

As for those caught up in prostitution, his attitude to women in general tells us that he would not have colluded in society's tendency to shun them. In fact, in a world that considered women to be inferior to men, Jesus treated them as equals. He also disregarded the purity laws (for example, in the story of the woman with a flow of blood), which declared prostitutes to be unclean. Jesus' attitude was highly unconventional, to say the least. God's message of love and redemption is for all humanity, and not just for a religious elite.

Paul and Prostitution

In the Graeco-Roman world, prostitution was widespread. Prostitutes, who were usually slaves, worked in brothels and bathhouses, and it was considered quite usual for men to make use of their services. Indeed, at civic and religious festivals and ceremonies prostitutes were often provided as part of the entertainment. In the first letter to the Corinthians, however, Paul says, in no uncertain terms, that this kind of behavior is out of bounds for Christian men.

> Do you not know that your bodies are members of Christ? Should
> I therefore take the members of Christ and make them members
> of a prostitute? Never! (1 Cor 6:15)

The question we have to ask is *why* does he object so strongly? To answer it we have to look at the broader context of the letter. Paul is answering some questions that the Corinthians have sent to him regarding problems that have come up in the church. What leader should they follow? How should they deal with disputes in the church? Earlier in chapter 6, he deals with the fact that some believers in Corinth are taking other believers to court. In this section, it seems that some in the congregation thought that they could do whatever they wanted with their bodies. They thought they could indulge their appetites, eat what they liked, and sleep with whomever they liked, because one day the body would be destroyed (6:12–13). Paul, however, is far from happy with this idea, and he gives several reasons why.

First, their bodies will not be destroyed at all, but be raised up at the end times (6:14). Just as God raised Jesus up, so He will raise them up too. Second, being a follower of Christ means that their bodies are not "just" their bodies, they are actually members of Christ (6:15). They are somehow joined to Christ, even a part of him. It is unthinkable that Christ's body be joined with a prostitute, so they cannot do whatever they want with their bodies. Thirdly, they are not only physically joined with Christ, they are also spiritually joined with him (6:17). So for a believer, sex is not just physical, it is also a spiritual thing in which something far more mysterious happens than the mere joining together of two bodies. It means they become "one flesh"—they have a spiritual union. And this means that indulging in transient sexual relationships risks damaging their relationship with Jesus Christ.

For the Christian men at Corinth, then, going to prostitutes was not merely a matter of entertainment, as they might have been accustomed to think, it is a spiritual matter, as we have seen. Not only that, it is a community matter, for what one man does with his body not only affects him as an individual, but also has an impact on the community as a whole. (12:12–13). The Corinthian men were therefore in a difficult situation—they were disciples of Christ, but at the same time they had to live in a pagan society, and there would always be the temptation to return to their old way of life, especially if they had business or family ties which meant they had to deal with non-believers. Christ had redeemed them from their sinful past, but, like the Israelites in the desert after their release from Egypt, they had to learn how to live with that freedom, and not be tempted by idolatrous (i.e., pagan) behavior (1 Cor 10:7; Exod 32).

Paul is insistent that men should not use prostitutes, and in this sense he introduces a new element into what the Bible has to say about prostitution: men should exercise self-control when it comes to their sexual behavior—because they are followers of Christ. And in a move that is remarkable for his time, Paul says that men, not just women, are a source of pollution for the community. He does not, however, say anything about prostitutes themselves, probably because this is not directly relevant to the problem at Corinth. He is only concerned with the behavior of the men, because that is what he has been asked about. We can therefore only infer what his attitude would be to those caught up in prostitution from what he says about sexual behavior in general. Given that he thinks marriage is the joining together of two people in a spiritual as well as physical way, and given his view that all believers are joined together as the body of Christ, we might expect that he would think that it would be harmful for Christian women to become involved in prostitution in the same way as for men.

Presumably, too, if a woman in prostitution became a Christian, she would be expected to stop her activities. This would mean that the community would have to help support her, as alternative work may not have been easy to find. However, most prostitutes were slaves, and as such they would not have the option of coming to church, let alone stopping work, without their owners' permission. If, somehow, a slave prostitute became a follower of Jesus, she would most likely have had to continue her work in the brothel or bathhouse, in the same way that many trafficked women and girls have to do today. It would certainly not be a loving Christian community that excluded someone in this situation.

Rahab and Tamar

In Matthew chapter 1, the Gospel is introduced with the genealogy of Jesus. The remarkable thing is that both Rahab and Tamar are included in it. Tamar is mentioned in 1:3 and Rahab in 1:5. Tamar is said to be the mother of Perez and Zerah. Rahab is the mother of Boaz. They are all ancestors of David and therefore ancestors of Jesus himself. As many have pointed out, it is truly remarkable that two women who are associated with prostitution are mentioned in Jesus' family tree. Once again, these two women, viewed as outcasts by their own people, are cited as important for God's work in history. Thus, in the New Testament, as in the Old, there is a voice that speaks of the dishonored person as honorable in God's sight.

We do not hear any more of Tamar after this. Rahab, however, is mentioned twice more in the New Testament, and each time, she is cited with honor. In Hebrews 11:31 it is extraordinary that she appears in the same list as people like Abraham, Jacob, and Moses. Like them she is an exemplar of faith, because of her hospitality to the spies, who were technically her enemies. In James 2:25 the subject is also faith, and the author is keen to emphasize the link between faith and actions. For example, Abraham was justified by offering his son Isaac as a sacrifice. James continues,

> You see that a person is justified by works and not by faith alone. Likewise, was not Rahab the prostitute also justified by works when she welcomed the messengers and sent them out by another road?

It is remarkable that their association with prostitution seems not to exclude them from these lists, but to be a primary reason for their inclusion. As in the Old Testament, it is recognized that God works through those whom society thinks beyond the pale.

The Whore of Babylon

The last passage in the New Testament in which a prostitute is mentioned is in Revelation 17 and 18. There we meet the Whore of Babylon. She is part of John's vision of the things that are to come in the future. We are told at the beginning of chapter 17 that John will be shown the judgment of the great whore. This astonishing figure sits on a scarlet beast that is full of blasphemous names. The beast has seven heads and ten horns. The woman wears rich clothes and jewelry. She holds in her hand a golden cup said to be full of abominations and the impurities of her fornication, and she is drunk on the blood of believers. She has a name written on her forehead: "Babylon the great, mother of whores and of earth's abominations." This woman has become very rich and kings throughout the world want to share her power. But she is no dignified woman. Rather, she is a revolting figure, stained with the blood of the martyrs. She thinks no one can conquer her, but she has in fact lost all sense of human decency—even to the extent of profiting from human trafficking (Rev 18:13). But she will be destroyed. The beast, which represents all the evil power that gives the whore her success, will turn on her. We are told in 17:16 that the beast and the kings who are at war with Jesus the Lamb, will hate the whore, and will turn on her, making her "desolate and naked." They will eat her flesh and burn her. Only those who have profited from her wealth and power will be sorry that she is gone.

What is going on in this strange passage? Although there have been many differing interpretations over the centuries, most scholars today think that the Whore of Babylon represents the Roman Empire in the first century CE. The book was probably written during the reign of the Roman Emperor Domitian (81–96 CE). Its aim is to encourage believers in Asia Minor (the area we know as Turkey today), who are suffering under the Roman Empire. Rome has become evil, greedy, and corrupt, and ordinary people are suffering as a result. Those who are willing to follow these corrupt ways may make a lot of money. The slave trade has flourished. Christians are being persecuted. Unscrupulous merchants have become very rich indeed. John, however, wants to reassure the Christians: one day this empire will fall and God's kingdom will be established. And in the meantime Christians must have nothing to do with her corrupt ways (Rev 18:4). She may think she is invincible, but they know that this is not true. One day, the bride of the Lamb, the exact opposite of the whore, will be seen "dressed in fine linen, bright and pure" (19:8). The whore will meet a terrible end, and so will the empire she represents.

Prostitution the in the New Testament

In Jesus' teaching, prostitutes are mentioned amongst the outcasts and the poor, as examples of those whom the religious establishment despises, but who are honored in God's kingdom. Prostitution is clearly seen as part of a world of sin, and those caught up in it are living lives that are hardly compatible with the will of God for his people. However, Jesus does not make any distinction between sexual sin and other types of sin, and he seems to be far more concerned with the hypocritical attitudes that cause the religious establishment to despise prostitutes as unrighteous and shameful, while believing that it enjoys God's favor. In fact, precisely the opposite is the case: the outcast and poor are those who are honored in God's kingdom—those who believe themselves righteous are not.

Jesus thus continues the tradition whose voice we have already heard in the Old Testament, which questions the values of the world. He exposes the self-serving thinking of those in authority. This same voice is given expression in the genealogies in which Rahab and Tamar are honored as ancestresses of Jesus, and in the remarkable fact that Rahab (who is always remembered as a prostitute) is considered to be an example of faith in both James and Hebrews. Those whom society thinks shameful can play crucial roles in the kingdom of God and be used to further his purposes. Paul's teaching is also remarkable. Christian men are to be a challenge to the cultural norms of their society and to take responsibility for their own sexual behavior. No longer are women solely to blame for the sexual sins of men.

So it seems that in the New Testament there are voices of redemption and love for those caught up in prostitution, voices that can still speak to us today. We must not despise those in prostitution, but nor should we go to the other extreme and view prostitutes as particular sinners, especially loved by God. This idea, which has been the basis for many a Christian's involvement in ministry to women in prostitution, is founded not on the New Testament itself, but on centuries of imaginative embellishment of the stories in the Gospels. What these stories do tell us, however, is of the respect and equality that Jesus affords to all women, something that was unheard of in his day, and indeed, often in our own.

This leaves us with one last question. What about the Whore of Babylon? Where is the voice of love and redemption in this passage, with its horrible lurid picture of a prostitute drinking the blood of martyrs and her terrible fate? Isn't this a voice of hatred and revenge, of violence and punishment? This, of course, is the same question that troubled us with regard to the Old Testament prophets' use of the prostitution metaphor to speak about idolatry. Indeed the Apocalypse's use of the idea of the whore is directly drawn from this prophetic tradition. And the answer that we gave there holds true here too. If we were to infer from this passage that prostitutes should be treated harshly and even killed, we would misunderstand the kind of literature we are reading and the message it is trying to convey.

The book of Revelation is an example of a particular kind of writing that was commonly used in the first-century Jewish world. Known to us today as "Apocalyptic" literature, it was designed to make the point that, even in the face of terrible evil and suffering, God's love will ultimately triumph. Fantastic images of beasts and dragons, battles and floods and fire are intended to have maximum effect on the reader's (or, more accurately, the listener's, for it would have been read aloud in the churches) imagination, driving home the message of how seriously God views sin and encouraging his people to persevere. The whore of Babylon is one such image, and she is not to be seen as a real person, but a symbol of the great evil, corruption, and idolatry that are characteristic of the Roman Empire. The passage, therefore, has nothing whatsoever to say about how we should respond to those caught up in prostitution, but it has a great deal to say about the greed and corruption which degrades those who try to gain as much for themselves as possible, and which results in all sorts of sinful behavior, including human trafficking.

Conclusion

What does all this have to say to us about contemporary sex trafficking? First, it means that it is quite natural for Marika to feel shame as a result of her experiences: she has been made to live in a way that is not true to the standards she has for herself. However, Christians should not add to her suffering. She and the many thousands of women and men who find themselves forced to work as prostitutes should be as welcome in our churches as anyone else. We are *all* sinners, loved by God. Second, we should be aware of our tendency to be fascinated by all things of a sexual nature—for whenever sex is brought into the picture, things tend to become complicated. Contrary to our expectations, the New Testament has remarkably little to say about prostitution, and the idea that the sin of those who work as prostitutes is worse than any other sin is not to be found there. In fact, Jesus himself is far more concerned with religious hypocrisy, greed, and the exploitation of the poor than with sexual sin. Third, Christians should be careful not to collude in attitudes that promote double standards. Primarily this means seeing men and women as equals, as Jesus himself did, and working against any tendencies to blame women for the sins of men. As Paul makes clear, men are responsible for their own sexual behavior. As far as legislation against sex trafficking is concerned, all this suggests that Christians should be supportive of the current moves to target the customers and the men and women who run the sex industry, rather than criminalizing prostitutes, as is often the case. Changing our attitudes in this way could be the beginning of freedom and change for many who have been victimized.

In the New Testament there are echoes of cultural voices that stigmatize those caught up in prostitution, along with subversive voices which challenge them. God continues to surprise us by honoring those whom the world thinks shameful. Above all, however, the voice of love and redemption is loud and clear. Jesus Christ has come to set the captives free—and that includes those whom the world thinks beyond the moral pale: prostitutes, pimps, and their clients. But that voice also continually sounds a warning to the disciples of Jesus. It is right that we speak out and work against the suffering and injustice that is human trafficking. But we must also be on constant guard against the temptation to think ourselves morally superior to others. For as soon as we do so, we fall into hypocrisy and idolatry ourselves.

 Questions for discussion.

1. What attitudes to people who work in prostitution have you come across? What is your own attitude?

2. Read 1 Corinthians 6. Why should men not use prostitutes? What does Paul's teaching tell us about Christian attitudes to sexual behavior in general?

3. Think about the story recounted in Brock and Nakashima's book *Casting Stones*. Would the presence of people who work in prostitution "spoil the image" of your church? How do you think the members of your church would react if people who work in prostitution came to your church?

4. Why do you think the figure of Mary Magdalene has been so fascinating throughout Christian history?

5. Jesus works against cultural norms and treats women equally to men, even giving them leading roles in his ministry. What attitudes towards women are to be found in your culture and/or community?

6. Many today argue that prostitution should be legalized and considered a profession like any other. What do you think of this idea, and what are the biblical grounds for your answer?

7. The prostitutes who are mentioned in the Bible are all women. We know, however, that there are many men and transgendered people who work in the sex industry. Does this make any difference to our Christian response?

8. Read Revelation 17–18. In this passage John is speaking in a way very similar to the Old Testament prophetic passages we looked at in the previous chapter. How do you think the figure of the whore of Babylon should be understood today?

8

CONCLUSION

Human Trafficking and the Bible:
Listening for the Voice of Love and Redemption

THE CENTRAL MESSAGE OF the Bible is of a redeeming God who sets the captives free. However, as the history of the church shows, it is remarkably easy to miss the voice that proclaims this message. We have to listen carefully for the voice of love and redemption in Scripture, for sometimes we can allow other voices to drown it out. As we have seen, it is easy to read the Bible with an unconscious desire to prop up our own firmly held beliefs, or to resist change. We need constantly to examine our motives as we read Scripture. Are we open to the voice of love and redemption, or are we seeking to maintain our own comfort and certainties, more interested in being right than in the risky business of obeying God's command to identify with the poor and oppressed, and to set the captives free?

With regard to slavery, several strands of tradition are preserved in the Old Testament. One strand tells us about the customs and practices of everyday life at various times in ancient Israel. It reflects the human attitudes and cultures that determined the way they lived. Thus, we find that the Israelites kept slaves, just as everyone else did. Another strand of tradition bears witness to attempts to curtail slavery within the people of Israel. While we might feel disappointed that they were unable to extend this to people of other nations and races, the important thing for us to note is that they were thinking through the implications of their belief that God had brought them out of captivity in Egypt. In addition, there are voices that contest these values and practices. For example, the commonly held view that some people in society are worthless meets with opposition in certain narratives, and in the wisdom literature. Various voices insist that slaves do not lose their dignity as human beings, and that God can use even those whom society discounts. The idea that we can oppress the poor and vulnerable is frequently challenged throughout the Old Testament by what I have called the voice of love and redemption, and is given its most powerful expression in the story of the exodus.

Just as the people of Israel had to learn to live as God's people, so too the early Christians had to learn to be disciples of Jesus. Thus, in the New Testament, we can hear certain voices that reflect their struggles to live as the church in a hostile world. However, the voice of love and redemption is to be heard loud and clear in the message of Jesus the redeemer, and it becomes obvious that if we want to be his followers, much is demanded of us. Not only are we to challenge the values of the world and work to "set the captives free," we are to embody Christ's upside-down values in our lives.

We are to consider ourselves as his slaves, living lives that identify with the weak, the oppressed, and exploited, rather than with those who are rich and powerful. In other words, we are to exemplify the ethos of love and redemption in our own lives. It is simply not an option for those who call themselves disciples of Christ to ignore the suffering of the exploited and oppressed.

With regard to sex-trafficking it is important to recognize that, historically, Christian attitudes towards those who are caught up in prostitution have contributed to their suffering. These attitudes continue today. In many parts of the world people in prostitution are still excluded from the church. Perhaps in reaction to this tendency, some Christians have felt a special sense of pity for victims of sex trafficking, believing that the Bible makes "special cases" of women who are caught up in prostitution. In the light of these conflicting responses, it is crucial that we have a clear understanding of what a "biblical" view of prostitution might be.

In ancient Israel, as in all societies, there were double standards. Women were blamed for breaking the sexual conventions (including working in prostitution), while men were apparently able to do what they wanted. However, some Scriptural voices challenge this, subtly mocking the idea that men could behave in any way they liked, or that they were necessarily more powerful and cleverer than women. In fact, those who are thought to be morally unacceptable turn out to be the very ones God uses to rescue his people, because of the mistakes made by those who are the more powerful in society! Conventional ideas of what is shameful are continually undermined in the Old Testament. We are constantly challenged to look beyond what seems so obvious on the surface and to expose hypocrisy and double standards. It is easy to go along with the crowd, and not to question cultural norms and attitudes—but Scripture invites us to do precisely the opposite.

When we turned to the New Testament we discovered that it has far less to say about prostitution than we might have expected. The traditional idea that Mary Magdalene was a prostitute, for example, turns out to be really much more to do with Christian imagination than anything the Bible has to say. Jesus has little or nothing to say about prostitution—he is much more concerned with the behavior of the religious leaders. He directly challenges the way society treats women in general, and he does not adhere to the purity laws, which were so important for ensuring that women in prostitution were deemed to be unclean. God's redemption is for all.

Paul challenges double standards. For the first time, men are instructed to exercise self-control, because of their new identity in Christ. They must not conform to cultural expectations.

It is interesting to notice that in the first century, if a slave-girl became a Christian, she would have had to continue her work as a prostitute. For the church, what is shameful is the fact that men are prepared to buy sex from her, not that she works in a brothel. Rahab and Tamar are honored as ancestresses of Jesus himself. The image of the whore of Babylon in Revelation is about the Roman Empire, and does not have anything to say to us about people in prostitution or how we should respond to them. Ultimately, however, the message of Revelation is that Jesus Christ will defeat the evil powers that seem to hold his people in thrall.

Once we have learned to listen for the voice of love and redemption, the message of Scripture is clear. Slavery is incompatible with all that we know of God's love for his people. Christians must stand up against the injustice that causes the suffering of people like Mende Nazir and Marika. As the slaves of Christ, we must stand by them and work for their freedom.

Slavery is caused and perpetuated by greed—greed for money and power. It is caused by people who take advantage of and exploit the poor. Human traffickers (as the writers of the New Testament knew) make money out of these desires, feed on the corruption that keeps these systems of power in place, and play to the greed that turns other people into commodities to be bought and sold. Christians can speak out against this.

Christians are not exempt from these temptations. We live in a world that is dominated by the powers of materialism and status. And as we have seen, change takes a long time to come about. Christians are no different from other people—they have their own lives to live, families to protect, careers to pursue. But the suffering and injustice of slavery demands that we do something about it. Throughout the world many Christians are actively involved in working against slavery: they are involved in rescue work, prevention, lobbying, and awareness-raising. But the Bible teaches that living for the redeeming God means that every aspect of our lives and values must be in accordance with our identities as slaves of Christ, and urges us to challenge the values of the world. Thus it is that all Christians are called to challenge the systems and values that perpetuate slavery. Not all are called to specific tasks of rescue work or lobbying, but we are all called to live prophetic lives, lives that speak of the love of God for all his people and his hatred of injustice and exploitation of the poor. For, the existence of slavery is an affront to all that Christianity represents—the redeeming God who sets the captives free.

Discussion Points for an Anti-Trafficking Mindset within the Church

In this last section I will make some suggestions that arise from our study of Scripture. They range from ideas about our calling as Christians to work against slavery to practical ideas as to how this can be done, and are offered, not as instructions, but for thoughtful consideration in discussion groups, and by individuals. Please consider them carefully and prayerfully, and think about how you and your community can work towards the eradication of slavery.

Human Trafficking in General

- We speak out with a prophetic voice against corruption and injustice when we see it.

- As "slaves of Christ" we identify with those who are least honorable in society.

- As "slaves of Christ" we are called to resist the forces in our world that urge us to seek power and wealth.

- The call to antislavery work is a natural outcome of our identity as "slaves of Christ."

- Christians have been set free, but that freedom is not without boundaries—we live under the Lordship of Jesus Christ.

- Our moral response to our gift of freedom is encapsulated in the "Golden Rule" (Matt 7:12).

- We refuse to collude in systems that exploit the vulnerable and poor.

- We challenge cultural practices and attitudes that contribute to the perpetuation of slavery (e.g., the caste system, discrimination against women).

- We need to find ways of providing just employment for those who are at risk of exploitation.

Sex Trafficking

- We must not add to the suffering of those who are, or have been, forced to work in prostitution, by seeing them as shameful or impure.
- We resist the argument that the "sex trade" should be legalized. The sex trade is undesirable because of its faulty views of the body and sexual relationships.
- We support the movement that insists that those who wish to buy sex should be made to take responsibility for the existence of prostitution.
- We consider ways to enable victims of sexual exploitation to be able to find alternative employment (e.g., the decriminalization of prostitution, encouraging ethical business ventures).
- We speak out against the objectification of human beings for sexual exploitation.
- We work against the poverty which forces families to sell their children into prostitution.

Living as "Slaves of Christ"

- We resist the temptation to legalism, remembering always that "the letter kills and the Spirit gives life."
- We recognize and resist any tendency to be hypocritical and self-righteous.
- We resist the temptation to think that Christians are morally superior to others.
- We recognize that our own self-interest, our cultural viewpoint, our societal norms can make us blind to the demands of the gospel.
- We repent of cultural patterns within our communities that lead us to seek our own comfort, resist change, and place these over and above the command to reach out to the poor.
- We seek to hear the redemptive voice of love in Scripture.

- We acknowledge that we all come to Scripture with our own presuppositions and agendas.

- We acknowledge that it is easy to use the Bible to support our own viewpoint, and seek to be honest interpreters of Scripture.

- We never use the Bible to oppress others or for our own selfish agendas.

- It is the law of love that will bring about social change—not our need to be right, or to look after our own interests.

- We strive to see the "big picture" of Scripture, and to interpret its various books and passages in the light of the overall story of God's redemptive work in history.

Prayer

Lord Jesus, you came into this world as the slave-king, proclaiming freedom for the captives. We pray that you will enable us, your slaves, not to seek our own wealth and status, but to walk alongside the outcast and poor. We ask that you will help us to live lives worthy of our calling as disciples and that, by your Holy Spirit, you will enable us to work together to set the captives free.

Amen

BIBLIOGRAPHY

Bales, Kevin. *Understanding Global Slavery: A Reader.* Berkeley: University of California Press, 2005.

Bauckham, Richard. *The Bible in Politics.* London: SPCK, 1989.

Benezet, Anthony. *A Caution and Warning to Great Britain and Her Colonies, in a Short Representation of the Calamitous State of the Enslaved Negroes in the British Dominions.* Philadelphia: Henry Miller, 1766.

Callahan, Allan Dwight. *The Talking Book.* New Haven, CT: Yale University Press, 2006.

Carretta, Vincent, ed. *Unchained Voices: An Anthology of Black Authors in the English Speaking World of the 18th Century.* Lexington, KY: The University Press of Kentucky, 1996.

Dilwyn, William, and John Lloyd. *The Case of Our Fellow Creatures, the Oppressed Africans Respectfully Recommended to the Serious Consideration of the Legislature of Great Britain by the People called Quakers.* London: James Philips, 1783.

Horsley, Richard A. "The Slave Systems of Classical Antiquity and Their Reluctant Recognition by Modern Scholars." *Semeia: Slavery in Text and Interpretation* 83/84 (1998) 19–66.

Haskins, Susan. *Mary Magdalene: Myth and Metaphor.* London: Harper Collins, 1993.

Malarek, Victor. *The Natashas: The New Global Sex Trade.* London: Vision, 2004.

Morgan, Kenneth. *Slavery in America: A Reader and Guide.* Edinburgh: Edinburgh University Press, 2005.

Patterson, Orlando. *Slavery and Social Death: A Comparative Study.* Cambridge: Harvard University Press, 1982.

Ruston, Roger. *Human Rights and the Image of God.* London: SCM, 2004.

Stowe, Harriet Beecher. *Uncle Tom's Cabin.* 1852. Reprint. Knoxville, TN: Wordsworth Classics, 1995.

Wesley, John. *Thoughts upon Slavery.* London: R. Hawes, 1774.

APPENDIX: SUGGESTIONS FOR FURTHER READING

Stories of Human Trafficking

Bok. F., with Edward Tivnan. *Escape from Slavery: The True Story of My Ten Years in Captivity—and My Journey to Freedom in America.* New York: St Martin's Griffin, 2003.

Cadet, Jean Robert. *Restavec: Haitian Slave Child to Middle Class American.* Austin: University of Texas Press, 1998.

Forsyth, Sarah. *Slave Girl.* London: Blake, 2010.

Ivison, Irene. *Fiona's Story: A Tragedy of our Times.* London: Virago, 1997.

Jal, Emmanuel. *War Child: A Child Soldier's Story.* London: Abacus, 2010.

Nazer, Mende, and Damien Lewis. *Slave: The True Story of a Girl's Lost Childhood and Her Fight for Survival.* London: Virago, 2004.

Waugh, Louisa. *Selling Olga: Stories of Human Trafficking and Resistance.* London: Pheonix, 2006.

Reading the Bible

Bauckham, Richard. *The Bible in Politics.* London: SPCK, 1989.

Brueggmann, Walter. *The Book that Breathes New Life: Scriptural Authority and Biblical Authority.* Edited by Patrick D. Miller. Minneapolis: Fortress, 2005.

———. *Truth Speaks to Power: The Countercultural Nature of Scripture.* Louisville, KY: Westminster John Knox, 2013.

Fee, Gordon, and Douglas Stuart. *How to Read the Bible for All Its Worth.* Grand Rapids: Zondervan, 2003.

Goldingay, John. *Old Testament Theology vol. 3 Israel's Life.* Downers Grove, IL: IVP Academic, 2009.

Patte, Daniel. *Ethics of Biblical Interpretation: A Re-Evaluation.* Louisville, KY: Westminster John Knox, 1995.

Webb, William J. *Slaves, Women and Homosexuals: Exploring the Hermeneutics of Cultural Analysis.* Downers Grove, IL: IVP, 2001.

Wright, N. T. *Scripture and the Authority of God.* London: SPCK, 2005.

Books on Modern-Day Slavery

Bales, Kevin. *Disposable People: New Slavery in the Global Economy.* Rev. ed. Berkeley: University of California Press, 2000.

—————. *Ending Slavery: How We Free Today's Slaves.* Berkeley: University of California Press, 2007.

—————. *Understanding Global Slavery: A Reader.* Berkeley: University of California Press, 2005.

Brock, Rita Nakashima, and Susan Brooks Thistlethwaite. *Casting Stones: Prostitution and Liberation in Asia and the United States.* Minneapolis: Fortress, 1996.

Jewell, Dawn Herzog. *Escaping the Devil's Bedroom.* Oxford: Monarch, 2008.

Kara, Siddharth. *Sex Trafficking: Inside the Business of Modern Slavery.* New York: Columbia University Press, 2009.

King, Gilbert. *Woman, Child for Sale: The New Slave Trade in the Twenty-First Century.* New York: Chamberlain Bros., 2004.

Malarek, Victor. *The Natashas: The New Global Sex Trade.* London: Vision, 2004.

Miles, Glen, and Christa Foster Crawford, eds. *Stopping the Traffick: A Christian Response to Sexual Exploitation and Trafficking.* Eugene, OR: Wipf & Stock, 2014.

Saeed, Fouzia. *Taboo! The Hidden Culture of a Red Light Area.* Karachi: Oxford University Press, 2003.

Shelley, Louise. *Human Trafficking: A Global Perspective.* New York: Cambridge University Press, 2010.

Ethics

Birch, Bruce C., and Larry L. Rasmussen. *Bible and Ethics in the Christian Life.* Minneapolis: Augsburg, 1988.

Hauerwas, Stanley. *The Peaceable Kingdom: A Primer in Christian Ethics.* South Bend, IN: University of Notre Dame Press, 1984.

Yoder, John Howard. *The Politics of Jesus: Vicit Agnus Noster.* 2nd ed. Grand Rapids: Eerdmans, 1994.

Fiction

Stowe, Harriet Beecher. *Uncle Tom's Cabin.* 1852. Reprint. Knoxville, TN: Wordsworth Classics, 1995.

Unigwe, Chika. *On Black Sisters' Street.* London: Vintage, 2009.

History

Carretta, Vincent, ed. *Unchained Voices: An Anthology of Black Authors in the English Speaking World of the 18th Century.* 1996. Reprint. Lexington, KY: University Press of Kentucky, 2004.

Equiano, Oloudah. *The Interesting Narrative and Other Writings*. 1789. Reprint. London: Penguin, 2003.

Noll, Mark A. *The Civil War as a Theological Crisis*. Chapel Hill, NC: University of North Carolina Press, 2006.

Pollock, John. *Wilberforce*. Berkhamstead, UK: Lion, 1977.

Piper, John. *Amazing Grace in the Life of William Wilberforce*. Wheaton, IL: Crossway, 2006.

Websites

www.antislavery.org
www.coatnet.org
www. justiceandcare.com
www.stopthetraffik.org
www.freetheslaves.net
www.tearfund.org/en/no child taken
www.europeanfreedomnetwork.org
www.ijm.org
www.ebf.org/anti-trafficking-materials

Made in the USA
Middletown, DE
29 May 2019